A Concise Introduction to Tibetan Buddhism

A Concise Introduction to
Tibetan Buddhism

John Powers

Snow Lion Publications
Ithaca, New York

Snow Lion Publications
P.O. Box 6483
Ithaca, NY 14851 USA
(607) 273-8519
www.snowlionpub.com

Printed in the USA on acid-free recycled paper.
Designed and typeset by Gopa & Ted2, Inc.

ISBN-13: 978-1-55939-296-9
ISBN-10: 1-55939-296-7

Library of Congress Cataloging-in-Publication Data

Powers, John, 1957-
A concise introduction to Tibetan Buddhism / John Powers.
p. cm.
Includes bibliographical references and indexes.
ISBN-13: 978-1-55939-296-9 (alk. paper)
ISBN-10: 1-55939-296-7 (alk. paper)
1. Buddhism—China—Tibet. 2. Tibet (China)—Religion. I. Title.
BQ7604.P688 2008
294.3'923—dc22
2007052611

Table of Contents

Technical Note

In keeping with the introductory nature of this work, technical terms have been kept to a minimum. Some Tibetan words have been spelled phonetically and treated as English words, while others have been given English translations. The first occurrence of the most important technical terms is accompanied by an italicized transliteration in parentheses. All other terms, as well as names, places, and titles of texts are given in indexes, along with their transliterated spellings. The transliteration follows the system of Turrell Wylie, which he describes in his article "A Standard System of Tibetan Transcription" (*Harvard Journal of Asiatic Studies* 22 [1959], pp. 261–76).

Phonetic spellings of terms, names, and places have been adopted for the benefit of nonspecialists, who are often bewildered by the many unpronounced consonants found in Tibetan and by the subtleties of Tibetan pronunciation. Most words have been phoneticized in accordance with the dialect of Lhasa, the capital of Tibet and its cultural and religious center. Pronunciations of these words vary greatly in other parts of Tibet, but the Central Tibetan pronunciation was chosen as the most commonly accepted standard. Some familiar terms have been rendered in accordance with their common spelling, for example Bön and Sakya. In this edition I have adopted umlauts and accent marks to facilitate pronunciation of some Tibetan sounds. Thus, the ö in *chö* (the Tibetan equivalent of *dharma*) is pronounced as in German, and é in *rinpoché* is pronounced "ay." Many Tibetan teachers who teach and publish in the West have established transliterations of their names that are widely used (e.g., Lama Yeshe), and I have used these in this book instead of my own phonetic system.

Sanskrit and Pāli

Sanskrit was the *lingua franca* of intellectuals and religious authors in ancient India. The subcontinent had (and still has) a plethora of different language groups and dialects, and so Sanskrit functioned as a common mode of discourse. It is a highly developed linguistic system, capable of expressing philosophical concepts with great subtlety and precision, and it became the main literary medium for Mahāyāna Buddhism. The Buddha is said to have urged his followers not to write or translate texts in Sanskrit, preferring that they use vernaculars that could be widely understood by all classes of people, but after his death Buddhist authors increasingly moved toward Sanskritization, and the majority of influential Mahāyāna works are in Sanskrit (or in what is often referred to by scholars as "Buddhist Hybrid Sanskrit," which combines elements of various dialects). Pāli is a language that appears to be related to north Indian dialects, but contemporary scholars generally believe that it is a Sanskritized literary language which differs from other Indic dialects. It is the language of the Theravāda canon, the only complete Buddhist canon that survives in an Indic language. In the modern period, both Sanskrit and Pāli are often written in the Devanāgarī script, but in ancient India Sanskrit was expressed in many different writing systems. The Sanskrit and Pāli alphabets contain more letters than does English, and so a number of letters are commonly expressed by means of diacritical marks (or by combinations of Roman consonants or vowels). The rules of pronunciation are similar for both Sanskrit and Pāli.

i. Vowels and Diphthongs Used in This Book

letter	*pronunciation*
a	uh, as in fun
ā	ah, as in charm
i	ih, as in pin
ī	ee, as in seek
u	oo, as in sue
ū	ooh, as in school
e	ey, as in prey
o	oh, as in phone

ai	aye, as in time
au	ow, as in cow
ṛ	er, as in fur

For those interested in correct pronunciation, long vowels should take approximately twice as long to speak as short vowels; thus ā is slightly lengthened and emphasized when pronounced. In addition, it should be noted that emphasis is often different from what English speakers expect, and so maṇḍala, for example, is pronounced MUHN duh luh, and not mahn DAH la, as English speakers unfamiliar with Sanskrit often say it. The rules of Sanskrit pronunciation are too complex to explore in this section, but readers who are interested in learning them may consult the opening chapter of William Whitney's *Sanskrit Grammar* (Cambridge: Harvard University Press, 1975).

ii. Consonants

Sanskrit and Pāli have several types of consonants, which are divided into five classes: guttural, palatal, lingual, dental, and labial. These classes are based on where in the mouth the sound is made. Thus gutturals are made in the throat, palatals are made by touching the tongue to the palate, linguals are retroflex sounds made by curling the tongue inside the mouth and touching the bottom of the tip to the palate, dentals are made by touching the tongue to the teeth, and labials are made with the lips. The gutturals are: ka, kha, ga, gha, and ṅa. The palatals are: ca, cha, ja, jha, and ña. The linguals are: ṭa, ṭha, ḍa, ḍha, and ṇa. The labials are: pa, pha, ba, bha, and ma. Other letters that should be mentioned are: (1) the "sibilants" śa and ṣa, both of which are pronounced "sh," as in usher or shine; (2) *anusvāra* ṃ, which is pronounced either as m, as in *saṃsāra*, or as ng, as in *saṃgha*; and (3) *visarga* ḥ, which is silent. V is classified as a "labial semivowel" and is commonly pronounced like English w by modern Indians. Thus "Veda" is pronounced "Wayda." Ca is pronounced cha, as in chair (and so Yogācāra is pronounced "Yogahchahra"). The palatal ña is pronounced nya; other letters are pronounced like their English equivalents.

Introduction

Several years ago, I joined a group of spectators in a small building at the top of a hill with snow-covered mountains in the background. Four Tibetan monks in maroon robes stood around a table holding thin metal cones containing fine, colored sand which they used to construct a maṇḍala, a circular diagram that is used as a template for meditation. They had already been working for two days, and the maṇḍala took another day to complete. The monks followed a centuries-old pattern for their sand painting, and each part was meticulously crafted. After the last details had been completed, the monks surveyed their handiwork with obvious satisfaction.

The next day they gathered around the table wearing ceremonial robes, holding ritual implements, and after a short period of chanting began to dismantle it with no apparent regrets. They told the audience that Buddhism teaches that all phenomena are impermanent, and that their production and destruction of this work of art is an example of Buddhist attitudes toward mundane attachments. Some members of the audience gasped as they began to destroy the artwork that had been so meticulously crafted, but the only response from the monks was a smile.

This scene has been enacted countless times throughout the Tibetan cultural region, where initiates into Vajrayāna Buddhism—the dominant system practiced in Tibet, which involves extensive use of imagery and visualization—generally receive initiation from masters who use such sand maṇḍalas as a focal point for their instructions. Vajrayāna is often referred to as "Tantra" because it is based on texts that generally have the word "tantra" in their titles. They were mainly composed in India, and most claim to have been spoken by the historical Buddha although they represent a departure (in form and content) from earlier sermons attributed to him. The main emphasis of tantric Buddhism is transformation of the psycho-physical continuum of practitioners through extensive use of ritual, visualization, and manipulation of subtle energies.

What made this scene noteworthy was the fact that the venue was a small liberal arts college in upstate New York, and all the spectators were non-Buddhists from the college and the surrounding area who came to see a colorful artistic performance from an exotic foreign culture. Every day of the monks' visit hundreds of people came to the college, where they were entertained by dance and chanting performances, as well as the spectacle of the maṇḍala's construction.

During breaks the younger monks generally spent their time in the college's video-game room, loudly competing with students and each other. Their favorite games involved gunfire and car racing. Several people remarked that they were surprised that the young monks were normal teenagers and at how easily they interacted with the students. Clearly they expected them to be too immersed in spiritual pursuits to have any interest in such mundane diversions as video games. The interactions between Western spectators and Tibetan monks is an important aspect of such performances, which are occurring with increasing frequency. Every year several troupes of monks tour Western countries to raise funds for their monasteries in India or Nepal and to spread Tibetan religion and culture. They also provide a venue to discuss the plight of Tibet under Chinese occupation and garner support for the cause of a free Tibet.

The Chinese invasion and occupation of Tibet in the 1950s and subsequent oppression prompted hundreds of thousands of Tibetans to flee their homeland and establish a new society in diaspora. From there Tibetan culture has been exported all over the world, and this small population (about six million worldwide) has been remarkably successful in attracting media interest and in making the world aware of the plight of Tibetans in occupied Tibet. Their culture is frequently depicted (not always in ways they approve) in Western movies, television, and documentaries. Their spiritual leader, the Dalai Lama, is a Nobel Peace Prize laureate and an international celebrity who regularly meets and talks with world leaders, despite the strenuous objections of the Chinese government, for whom he is a constant source of embarrassment. During his tours of Western countries, he regularly fills halls and auditoriums that hold tens of thousands of people and that are normally used for sporting events and rock concerts.

At the same time, the situation in Tibet remains grim. Every year more than three thousand desperate Tibetans flee into exile, crossing some of the world's highest mountain passes and stretching the resources of the refugee community in India. Many lamas (the Tibetan translation of "guru," religious teacher) have established Buddhist centers in the West. Increasing numbers of Westerners have converted to Tibetan Buddhism, and thousands of Tibetan teachers now live in foreign countries. Tibetan religion and culture are being steadily destroyed in their land of origin but are enjoying unprecedented popularity around the world.

Despite the best efforts of the Chinese government to suppress Tibetan religion and culture, devotion remains strong among ordinary Tibetans, and decades of official vilification of the Dalai Lama have done little to diminish his appeal. A striking example of this was the response to his comments at a public religious ceremony in 2006 in which he condemned the popular Tibetan practice of wearing animal furs. He declared that the practice made him "ashamed" and urged Tibetans to recognize that killing animals for their fur is a violation of Buddhist principles. A number of Tibetans traveled to India to attend the ceremony, and when they returned and reported the Dalai Lama's comments, a wave of fur burnings swept through Tibet, much to the chagrin of Chinese authorities, who loudly proclaim his irrelevance and lack of popularity. The scale of the burnings and the almost total demise of the fur business in Tibet were in stark contrast to official pronouncements, and Chinese officials soon declared fur burning illegal. Much of the fur trade deals in skins of endangered animals; the Chinese government has vainly tried to curtail it, and so it was a major embarrassment that the exiled Buddhist leader was able to succeed so dramatically where they had failed.

Possession or display of photographs of the Dalai Lama or his writings can lead to lengthy prison terms, and state-run television, newspapers, and radio regularly carry scathing denunciations of his personality, morality, and religious position, but these have done little to diminish his appeal to his fellow Tibetans. He is a symbol for millions worldwide of genuine, unaffected happiness, wisdom, and compassion. Describing himself as "a simple Buddhist monk," he appears to have few pretensions, and his sense of humor and smile have won the hearts of hundreds of thousands who flock to his public lectures. Moreover, despite turning seventy in 2005, his energy and enthusiasm appear to be undiminished. He has a vigorous schedule of appearances all over the world and shows no signs of slowing down. Every time he accepts an invitation to visit a foreign country, the Chinese government attempts to pressure its government to prevent him from speaking publicly, but few countries heed threats of economic reprisals. His simple message of compassion and a "good heart" resonate even with non-Buddhists, and every public appearance leads to an upsurge of interest in Tibetan Buddhism.

The popularity of the Dalai Lama and other exiled Tibetan religious leaders has created a need for a concise introduction to Tibetan Buddhism. Along with increasing media attention, there has been a corresponding phenomenon of often bizarre claims about this tradition, as well as distorted notions, misinformation, and fantasy inventions that have little or no relation to their purported origin. Tibetan fantasies have a long history in the West, beginning in the fifth century B.C.E. with a report in Herodotus' history of huge ants on the Tibetan plateau that mined gold.

During the eighteenth and nineteenth centuries, European spiritualists often viewed Tibet as a repository of ancient wisdom. Among the most enthusiastic promoters of this notion was Helena Blavatsky, the founder of the Theosophical Society, who claimed that spiritual adepts called "Mahatmas" lived in remote areas of Tibet. They maintained ancient wisdom traditions in secret, but she claimed that they deposited written instructions in her cabinet. The fact that these had little or no relation to anything resembling Tibetan Buddhism only indicated to her that the true teachings of the masters were hidden even from their fellow Tibetans; but they were eager to share them with Europeans with no training or background in the system.

Tibetan fantasies continue to appear in the West. Tibet has been the backdrop for a number of popular works of fiction, perhaps most famously James Hilton's 1933 novel *Lost Horizon*, which depicted an idyllic land called Shangri-la nestled in a remote Tibetan valley. Here the best of world culture is preserved by wise lamas, but it turns out that their library and music collection appear to include only Western works. Moreover, the head of the monastery is revealed as a European, whom the locals have recognized as their natural leader. This was made into a Hollywood movie in 1937, and it has been followed by many others. Most depictions of Tibet present it as exotic and as a place that preserves wisdom that can benefit the West. An example of this attitude is the claim by rock star Sting that his life has been transformed by the practice of "tantric sex," despite the fact that he has no training in the system and lacks all of the basic prerequisites for initiates into tantric yogas.[1]

Sting claims that "tantric sex" provides him with many wonderful orgasms, but the sexual yogas of Vajrayāna were designed to facilitate the spiritual progress of advanced meditators seeking to attain buddhahood for the benefit of other beings and have nothing to do with sexual indulgence. Moreover, only adepts who have trained for many years and have attained a high level of control over subtle energies and advanced states of consciousness are given these esoteric instructions.

Some odd claims about Tibet turn out to be true. When I first heard that action movie star Steven Seagal—of such ultraviolent films as *Under Siege* and *Hard to Kill*—had been recognized as the reincarnation of a Tibetan lama, I assumed that it was another strange Tibetan fantasy, but the recognition was confirmed by Penor Rinpoche, at that time the supreme head of the Nyingma order. Since his recognition, he has reportedly devoted himself to the study of Tibetan Buddhism and to meditation, while at the same time continuing to make films that celebrate violence.

In light of the many fantastic representations of Tibetans, their religion, and their culture, there is a clear need for authoritative sources on the subject. My goal in writing this book is to present the essentials of the doctrines and practices of the tradition and to provide an overview of the teachings of its most influential figures.[2] Some readers will no doubt be disappointed

1 The sexual yogas of Vajrayāna and the prerequisites for this training are discussed in chapter 5, "Tantra."

2 Some portions of this book were previously published in my *Introduction to Tibetan Buddhism* (Ithaca: Snow Lion Publications, 1995; second edition 2007). At five hundred pages, it is too long for the attention spans of many contemporary readers, and the publisher has been urging me to write a condensed version for several years. This book is the result of a difficult process of condensing the material of the earlier book into a much smaller format. This has required that many difficult editorial decisions be made, resulting in the omission of a number of significant topics, eliminating whole chapters of the earlier book, and rewriting large sections in a condensed form. Readers who want more information on particular topics should consult *Introduction to Tibetan Buddhism* or works mentioned in the Bibliography.

that Tibetan Buddhism turns out to be less exotic than they had imagined, but I hope that the more fantastic notions about Tibet will be replaced by an appreciation for the richness of this ancient tradition and the profundity of its teachings.

1: The Indian Background

Origins of Tibetan Buddhism

SINCE the People's Republic of China invaded Tibet and annexed it to its growing empire in the 1950s, the government has waged a propaganda war aimed at convincing the Tibetan people and the rest of the world that Tibet was already a part of China since at least the twelfth century. Sending troops into the country, deposing the government of the Dalai Lama, and subsequent torture and killing of those who opposed these moves were characterized as "internal affairs," and foreigners were told that they were none of their business. In addition, China's position is that the Buddhism practiced in Tibet was largely imported from China—along with most other significant elements of Tibetan culture—and so Tibet was never an autonomous nation, but rather a province of China with intimate cultural connections to the rest of the country and under the direct control of the central government.

Tibetan historical accounts, however, tell a different story. Some Chinese teachers found followers in Tibet during the early period of Buddhism's spread into the region (beginning in the seventh century), but by far the most important influence was Indian forms of Buddhism that were mainly imported from the great monastic universities of northern India and Vajrayāna cults that mostly originated in Bengal and Bihar. Most of the major luminaries of the tradition are either Indian masters or indigenous teachers, but no Chinese Buddhists are considered important figures in the introduction or spread of Buddhism in Tibet. Tibetan monasteries contain numerous images and murals of Indian and Tibetan masters, but I have never seen any representations of Chinese figures. The most prominent symbol of Chinese Buddhism for most Tibetans is Hashang Mahayana (Chin. Heshang Moheyan), a Chinese Chan master who often appears in religious dances. He is a comic figure with a large round face and exaggerated Chinese features, who stumbles around and is prone to hurting himself. Tibetans find his antics hugely entertaining, and he is often connected with anti-Chinese sentiment among exile Tibetans, who view him as a representation of the country that invaded their homeland.

The Buddha

For contemporary Tibetans, the most enduring symbol of their religion is the Buddha, an Indian sage who probably lived in the fifth century B.C.E. and who was born in southern Nepal. According to tradition, his father, Śuddhodana, was the king of a small state whose capital city was Kapilavastu. His mother, Māyā, gave birth to him in a grove called Lumbinī, a short distance away, but she died soon afterward and he was raised by his stepmother, Prajāpatī.

The young prince was named Siddhārtha Gautama, and because he was born into the Śākya clan he is commonly referred to as Śākyamuni (Sage of the Śākyas). Shortly after his birth, his father consulted several astrologers to determine his future. He was told that the boy was exceptional and would one day be a great king. One astrologer concurred that the boy might pursue this path but stated that he could also decide to renounce the world as a wandering ascetic, in which case he would become a buddha. The term "buddha" means "awakened" and is based on the notion that most people spend their lives in ignorance of the true nature of reality, engaging in activities that they believe will result in happiness but that really lead to suffering and continued rebirth.[3] According to Buddhism, all beings are born over and over in a beginningless cycle, and the factor that keeps the process going is ignorance (*ma rig pa, avidyā*).[4] Their minds are conditioned to accept the conventional wisdom that acquiring wealth, fame, power, sex, etc. will lead

3 According to all schools of Buddhism, he was not the first buddha, nor will he be the last. In our era, he was preceded by six others, and he will be followed by another buddha, who will be named Maitreya.

4 In this book I have attempted to keep technical terms to a minimum. The Tibetan version of the term will appear first, followed by its Sanskrit equivalent.

to happiness, but even a cursory examination of the actual state of things reveals that those who most relentlessly pursue their own welfare tend to be friendless and unhappy. Conversely, people who work for the betterment of others and are motivated by sincere compassion and love tend to be content, even if they have little money and few resources. Buddhas are those who have fully awoken from the sleep of ignorance in which most beings spend their lives and who comprehend the true nature of reality.

They see that every action leads to an opposite and equal reaction, as Isaac Newton observed, and that this pattern pervades the entire universe. Every action (*las, karma*) that one performs produces concordant results, and one's present situation is a direct result of previous decisions and actions. All beings whose cognitions are conditioned by ignorance are caught up in cyclic existence (*'khor ba, saṃsāra*). Each life situation (whether one is beautiful or ugly, rich or poor, healthy or sickly) is influenced by the decisions of past lives, and the major events of one's present existence are similarly conditioned by the moral decisions one made in the past. The system is perpetuated by ignorance, which blinds beings to the realities of their situations and causes them to engage in counterproductive actions again and again. Buddhas, however, break free from past conditioning and examine the world as it really is, finding for themselves how things work and making decisions that lead to liberation from the vicious cycle of ignorance and suffering. Moreover, they also teach others what they have learned, and so open a path to liberation for countless beings who would otherwise be condemned to make the same mistakes and suffer their negative consequences.

Attainment of Buddhahood

One might expect that Siddhārtha's father would be thrilled to learn that his son could become such a savior for humanity, but traditional accounts report that he was appalled at the prospect of the prince renouncing his royal birthright and pursuing the path of a wandering holy man. The dissenting astrologer informed Śuddhodana that if Siddhārtha were to reach his maturity without becoming aware of the negative aspects of cyclic existence, he would remain in the world and devote himself to royal pursuits. If, however, he were to encounter a sick person, an old person, a corpse, and a world renouncer, he would realize the futility of mundane attachments and leave the palace, eventually finding the truth and becoming a buddha.

These four realities are referred to by Buddhists as the "four sights" and are representations of the primary negative aspects of ordinary existence: all beings are subject to sickness, all are constantly growing older and experiencing the progressive debilitating effects of this process, and all will eventually die. Along the way, suffering, loss, and disappointment may occur at any time, without warning, and no one is fully immune, no matter how well favored they appear to be.

Buddhists do not deny that there are possibilities for joy—nor do they dismiss the potential benefits of interpersonal relationships, family, a good job, or the pursuit of positive goals—but they hold that all such worldly entanglements are ultimately unsatisfactory (*sdug bsngal, duḥkha*). The term *duḥkha* is commonly translated as "suffering," but it encompasses a wide range of negative phenomena, including minor inconveniences, losses, and frustrations, as well as intense physical or mental trauma, along with separation from those things one desires and being forced to put up with situations that make one unhappy, bored, or upset. Life is full of frustrations, pain, loss, and ultimately ends in death, and so those who expect ordinary existence to produce lasting happiness for them are bound to be disappointed.

Buddhas, however, are able to transcend these negative realities and establish a lasting state of contentment. Through initially renouncing the world and its beguiling attractions, they pursue a path of inner meditation and cultivation of positive actions and eventually break the hold of ignorance. Even more importantly, they then teach others what they have learned and provide them a path to reach a state of liberation from cyclic existence.

In traditional accounts of Siddhārtha's life, he is said to have been immersed in the lifestyle of a prince and a member of the warrior caste.[5] His father surrounded him with beautiful women and ensured that he was involved in sporting contests, martial arts, and a range of entertainments. He ordered that no sick or old people be allowed in the palace, and when

5 The warriors and rulers (*kṣatriya*) are one of the four varṇas, or social groupings, of traditional Indian society. The kṣatriyas rank second in the hierarchy after brahmans (priests), and their traditional role was to be soldiers and rulers.

someone died the corpse was quickly removed before the prince could see it. World renouncers were similarly banned.

By keeping his son in the palace, Śuddhodana ensured that he only saw the best of what the world could offer a young prince, but in his midteens Siddhārtha asked to be allowed to see the kingdom that he would one day rule. Initially reluctant to let him encounter the uncertainties of the outside world, the king eventually relented but ordered that all examples of the "four sights" be removed from the prince's route. Despite his efforts, shortly after leaving the palace, Siddhārtha's chariot was halted by a sick man slowly making his way across the road. Never having encountered serious illness, the prince asked how he came to be in such a condition and was informed that sickness afflicts all beings. On subsequent trips he saw an old man leaning heavily on his cane and showing the debilitating effects of age and a corpse being carried through the streets by grieving friends and relatives. Upon learning that such conditions afflict all beings, the prince expressed amazement that most people encounter such sights every day but continue to pursue lifestyles that ensure that they will be prone to suffering throughout their lives.

On his fourth journey outside the palace, the prince saw a world renouncer and was immediately impressed by his calm demeanor and the peaceful expression on his face. His charioteer Channa informed him that this was one of many seekers of liberation who wandered the Indian subcontinent, practicing meditation and various austerities in the hope of putting an end to suffering. At this point Siddhārtha realized his true calling, and upon returning to the palace informed his father and wife Yaśodharā that he intended to leave behind his privileged life and go into the forest, exchanging his royal robes for the simple garb of an ascetic. His family and friends attempted to talk him out of his decision, but he remained adamant, and one night after a prolonged celebration he looked at the revelers sprawled on the floor in unflattering positions, their limbs askew, their features distorted. The beauty of the palace courtesans was revealed to be the result of the artifice of makeup and concealment of physical flaws, and as they snored and drooled Siddhārtha was overcome by a profound revulsion for worldly pursuits.

As the palace slept, Siddhārtha roused his charioteer and said he wished to be driven to the edge of the wilderness, where he would begin his career as a wandering ascetic. He left the opulence of the palace without any regrets, and despite the grief of his pregnant wife and loving parents he decided to pursue a path that might lead to the ultimate good, which would benefit many beings.

He knew little of the lifestyle or practices of world renouncers and sought instruction from several teachers. He quickly mastered their meditative techniques, which resulted in attainment of blissful states of consciousness, but he recognized that these are ultimately pointless because they are transitory. Meditators who attain them only experience a brief respite from the harsh realities of life, but Siddhārtha was looking for a permanent solution to the problem of the unsatisfactoriness of cyclic existence.

He spent several years with five ascetics who believed that the path to lasting happiness involves severe physical renunciation. Like them, he engaged in extreme fasting and various painful physical regimens, but one day passed out from lack of energy. Upon awakening, he realized that excessive asceticism is just as much a trap as hedonism, and so he resolved to follow a "middle way" (*dbu ma'i lam, madhyama-pratipad*) between these two alternatives. This became a cornerstone of Buddhist practice, which rejects all extremes as ultimately counterproductive, and of Buddhist thought, which similarly characterizes polarized views as misguided.

Soon afterward, Siddhārtha ate a refreshing meal of sweet rice, which caused his companions to view him as a weakling who had succumbed to worldly delights. For his part, the former prince recognized that they were following a path that leads nowhere, and so he set off on his own to find a way to transcend suffering. He traveled to modern-day Bodh Gaya in the Indian state of Bihar, where he sat under a tree (referred to by Buddhists as the "Tree of Awakening"). He entered into progressively more profound meditative states, and he realized how things come to be, how everything in the universe arises from causes and conditions, how things change from moment to moment, and how all things pass away.

As his insight expanded, he was able to perceive the events of his past lives and understand how his actions had provided the conditions for subsequent experiences. He then comprehended this process on a universal scale and directly perceived the actions of other beings and their results. During the night, the final vestiges of ignorance were removed, and at dawn he experienced the final awakening of a buddha. According to Tibetan Buddhism, from this point he was fully omniscient and possessed supernatural powers well beyond those of gods. Moreover, he was able to see directly into the minds of others and possessed a unique skill that enabled him to teach each person he encountered in the most beneficial way.

The First Sermon

Following his attainment of buddhahood, Siddhārtha remained sitting under the Tree of Awakening for several days, enjoying the experience of total freedom and ultimate awareness. He then decided to share what he had realized with others. His former ascetic companions were chosen as the recipients for his first public teachings because through his supranormal perception he realized that despite following a path that cannot lead to liberation they were very close to the truth. He traveled to Sarnath, a small village near modern-day Varanasi where they were staying, but when he approached they at first resolved to ignore him as a failed ascetic who had lost his resolve. As he drew nearer, however, they recognized a profound change in his demeanor and despite themselves asked about his aura of wisdom and serenity. He informed them that since his departure he had experienced the full realization of a buddha and that he was now completely free from the snares of cyclic existence. The ascetics asked him to teach them his new-found dharma (Tib. *chos*; a term encompassing Buddhist thought and practice), and he responded by delivering a short sermon that is now known as "The Discourse Turning the Wheel of Dharma." This is viewed as the beginning of the Buddha's teaching career, and it set in motion a series of instructions on various topics designed to lead his audiences toward realization of the truth he had discovered in Bodh Gaya.

The Four Noble Truths

He first taught them the "middle way" and explained that severe asceticism is a trap for seekers of liberation. He then described the situation of ordinary beings within cyclic existence in a set of propositions referred to by Buddhists as the "four noble truths": (1) suffering; (2) the cause of suffering; (3) its cessation; and (4) the path to overcoming suffering. The first holds that all life inevitably involves pain and various discontents. Suffering results from encountering unpleasant situations, from physical pain, from losing things that one values, and from the constant changes and shifts that are part of daily life. The second noble truth asserts that the root cause of suffering is desire: we want things to be different from what they are, and as a result we are disappointed. Humans in particular have many unrealistic expectations: that life will be fair; that they will prosper and get what they desire; that those one finds attractive will share this attraction; that they will live indefinitely; and so on. The inevitable clash between desires and expectations and reality is a constant source of frustration and dissatisfaction. If, however, one dispassionately examines the way things really are, one realizes that it is foolish to expect such things, and one gradually lowers expectations. The less one desires, the less prone one will be to suffering and conversely the more one's ability to appreciate the positive outcomes life offers will be enhanced.

The third noble truth maintains that there is a way out of the vicious cycle of desire, disappointment, loss, suffering, pain, and death. The way to transcendence of cyclic existence and its vicissitudes is the "eightfold noble path," which constitutes a set of principles for cognitive reorientation.

The eightfold path outlines a course of practice aimed at overcoming suffering. The root of suffering is desire based on ignorance, and the primary concern of the path is overcoming this underlying cause of all cyclic existence.

1. *Correct view* consists of both positive and negative aspects: on the positive side, it involves knowing certain key Buddhist concepts, such as the four truths and the operation of dependent arising, or understanding what actions lead to good and bad effects. It also entails eliminating wrong views, the most dangerous of which is the "view of true personhood" (*'jig tshogs la lta ba, satkāya-dṛṣṭi*), the conviction that the elements of the psycho-physical personality constitute a truly existent person. Wrong views are to be avoided, not merely because they are philosophically or logically untenable, but because they are conceptual manifestations of ignorance, desire, and aversion. Holding them leads to further desire, hatred, ignorance, and ultimately to further suffering.
2. *Correct intention* involves developing a proper orientation—that is, a mental attitude that aims at following the Buddhist path to awaken-

ing. In cultivating correct intention, a person decides what is ultimately important, what he or she will work at. In a Buddhist context, the ultimate goal is awakening, and a person who has correct intention will take this as the goal of religious activity. This decision is of fundamental importance, because in order to achieve something difficult (such as buddhahood) it is necessary to devote oneself to it single-mindedly. A person with correct intention cultivates an attitude of renunciation of worldly things, avoids harming others, and engages in activities that are concordant with the goal.

3. A person with *correct speech* avoids abusive, coarse, and untruthful words, says what is correct and true, and speaks gently and nonbelligerently. Since one's discourse is an outward manifestation of internal mental states, cultivating truthful and pleasant speech also leads to gradual development of concordant mental attitudes.
4. For monks and nuns, *correct action* involves keeping the rules of monastic discipline, and for laypeople it requires adherence to precepts which forbid killing, stealing, lying, sexual misconduct, and ingesting intoxicants. These rules are not simply arbitrary strictures, and they have a practical basis: cultivating morality results in mental calm, which is a prerequisite for later concentrations and advanced levels of consciousness. In order to attain the higher meditative states, one must overcome the mental troubles and disturbances that agitate the minds of ordinary beings and impede their ability to concentrate. Correct action is mainly concerned with avoiding the physical expressions of negative mental attitudes.
5. *Correct livelihood* is also connected with moral training: it consists in avoiding occupations that result in breaking the precepts—professions that lead people to kill, lie, cheat, steal, or engage in sexual misconduct. Prohibited occupations include hunting, fishing, meat-selling, making weapons, prostitution, and other activities that involve people in evil deeds.

The next three aspects of the path are concerned with meditation. A person who has cultivated the previous good qualities has created a foundation consisting of proper attitudes and actions. Based on morality and the calm mental states that it produces, a person has the prerequisites for pursuing the higher levels of meditative training.

6. *Correct effort* involves properly orienting the mind toward the desired goal of liberation. In this practice, a yogin overcomes negative feelings that inhibit equanimity and meditation, such as impatience, slothfulness, excessive pride, vengefulness, concern with unimportant things such as wealth, power, etc. The yogin then focuses on the goal of liberation through concentrated meditative practice. This involves steady effort rather than spurts of enthusiastic activity.
7. *Correct mindfulness* is emphasized in Buddhist meditation manuals as being of fundamental importance in meditation. In order to attain liberation, one must initially develop awareness of what one is doing and why one is doing it. In addition, one must learn to control and regulate the mind. A person seeking liberation must move from his or her present state of confusion and random thoughts to one of clarity and mindfulness in which he or she is aware of mental processes and attitudes and, more importantly, is in control of them.
8. *Correct concentration* requires the previous steps. Without a focused mind that can fix itself calmly and one-pointedly on a single object without being distracted, one cannot properly enter into the concentrations, which are advanced meditative states in which one's attention is fully devoted to an object of observation.

Taken together, the four noble truths constitute a summary of the Buddhist path. The truth of suffering indicates the basic problem that Buddhism proposes to overcome, and the truth of the origin of suffering shows the cause of the problem. The third truth holds that the negative elements of the human condition are not immutable, and the fourth truth indicates how a person may bring about a cognitive reorientation and transcend suffering.

The Buddha's Teaching Career

Upon hearing the Buddha's words, one of the ascetics named Kauṇḍinya became an *arhat* (Tib. *dgra bcom*; a person who has eliminated the major mental afflictions of desire, aversion, and obscuration and who will attain nirvana at the end of his or her life), and the others had profound realizations that established them on the Buddhist path to awakening. They asked to be allowed to become his disciples, and he initiated them as monks and thus established the Buddhist monastic order (*dge 'dun, sangha*).

From this point until the end of his life, the Buddha traveled around northern India, teaching all who came to him. According to Buddhist tradition, he was like a skilled physician, who could instantly analyze the spiritual illness of each patient and provide instructions that could alleviate the problem. This makes sense as spiritual therapy, but from a doctrinal standpoint it created difficulties for his later followers. The Buddhist canon contains a bewildering array of doctrines, discourses, and approaches, each of which was intended for a particular person or group. When the Buddha was alive, his followers could ask the master to reconcile contradictions or fill in the gaps, but after his death they had to sort through his teachings on their own and attempt to formulate a consistent presentation of his "real" thought. When asked near the end of his life how to distinguish between the "word of the Buddha" and spurious teachings that others might attribute to him after his death, he replied, "Whatever is well-spoken is the word of the Buddha."[6] In other words, if a particular teaching leads to virtuous action and to a decrease of suffering, and if it accords with empirical evidence, it may safely be adopted and practiced, no matter who originally propounded it.

The Buddha soon attracted a number of devoted followers, and the most dedicated became monks. He later instituted an order of nuns and also reportedly had numerous lay adherents. As the order grew, the need for rules and regulations became apparent, and this led to the development of a monastic code called the *vinaya* (Tib. *'dul ba*, literally "discipline"). This occurred in a mostly piecemeal fashion: the Buddha laid out a few simple rules for monastic conduct, but inevitably issues and disputes arose, and as each was brought to his attention, the Buddha issued an increasingly complex and detailed set of regulations that eventually produced a code governing all aspects of the lives and practice of the monastic community. Today there are several extant versions of the vinaya, including the Mūlasarvāstivāda Vinaya, which is practiced in the Tibetan cultural area, the Dharmaguptaka Vinaya, which is normative in East Asia, and the Theravāda Vinaya, which is followed by monks in Southeast Asia. The latter tradition is the only one

6 This statement is found in the *Uttaravipatti-sutta* (*Aṅguttara-nikāya* IV.163). This passage and its implications for Buddhist exegesis are discussed by George Bond in *The Word of the Buddha* (Colombo: M.D. Gunasena, 1982), p. 30ff.

whose complete canon exists today in an Indic language. The Theravāda canon is written in Pāli and so is commonly referred to as the "Pāli canon."

Entry into Final Nirvana

As he approached his eightieth year, the Buddha's body became increasingly frail, and he told his followers that he experienced constant pain in his back. During periods of meditation the pain was suspended, but it returned as soon as the meditation session was finished. He decided that he had fully imparted the dharma to his followers, holding nothing back, and this legacy would continue to be transmitted by them to others. His mission completed, he decided to enter nirvana (Tib. *mya ngan las 'das pa*, described in Buddhist texts as a state of perfect peace that transcends the sufferings of cyclic existence), and after a brief sermon exhorting his followers to pursue their practice with diligence, he passed away, surrounded by grieving disciples. His corpse was cremated, and the remaining relics were divided up. Some were interred in *stūpa*s (Tib. *mchod rten*; reliquary mounds that are popular throughout the Buddhist world), while others were given to devotees. The Buddha's relics and the stūpas originally built to house them later became focal points of Buddhist cultic practice.

Shortly after the Buddha's passing, some members of the monastic order became concerned that the teachings might die out or become distorted unless they were preserved, and so a council was convened to recite the Buddha's discourses and create a canon. Five hundred arhats who had been present when he taught were invited. The Buddha's personal attendant, Ānanda, recited from memory the Buddha's discourses, and the other arhats made minor corrections. Upāli—who was regarded as the greatest specialist in monastic discipline—recited the vinaya, and at the conclusion all agreed that the entire "word of the Buddha" had been codified and that from this point no new discourses would be accepted as authoritative.

Memories of the Buddha

The passing of the founder of a religious tradition often leaves a void in the community because there is no longer the possibility of daily guidance and personal inspiration. A common response is to develop a biography and regularly recount the paradigmatic deeds of the founder, whose life story is presented as a model for emulation by the faithful. In the case of the early Buddhist community, the memory of the Buddha was preserved by his disciples, who passed on their recollections of his words and deeds to others who had never met him. After the Buddha's death, his followers began recounting his story in order to inspire others. As time passed, the legend was embellished and augmented, with the result that a rich and detailed mythology developed. This has become a shared cultural legacy for Buddhists. The story highlights important aspects of their tradition and serves as a paradigm for devout practitioners.

By the time Buddhism reached Tibet, the historical Buddha had faded into the mists of the distant past, and the religion's founder mainly functioned as an important shared symbol. This symbol was understood and interpreted differently by different schools of Buddhism, each of which appropriated it in accordance with its own ideas, presuppositions, and practices. For each school, the Buddha's life and teachings were represented in a way that validated and corroborated its own doctrines and its own understanding of the methods and goals of Buddhist thought and practice.

Following the death of the Buddha, the tradition he founded began to develop different schools, many of which compiled their own versions of the canon, and each of which had its own understanding of the doctrines he propounded and the path to liberation that he showed his followers. In the following sections we will examine some of the most significant developments of Indian Buddhism and some of the most influential doctrines attributed to the Buddha.

2: Mahāyāna

Origins

In the centuries following Śākyamuni's death, numerous schools and subschools arose, some of which were identified by points of doctrine or monastic discipline, and others that were associated with particular regions. In addition, even after the death of the founder of the tradition, new texts continued to appear, many of which claimed to have been spoken by him. To make the situation even more confusing, older texts were being redacted, and new material was often added. In some cases, this textual development can be traced by examining the dated Chinese translations of a given work, which often indicate that as new ideas and models developed in India they were incorporated into existing texts.[7] Successive versions of a given text sometimes exhibit significant growth, as new ideas were incorporated into existing canonical sources in order to give them added validity. Since Buddhism has no centralized authority and no ecclesiastical body that oversees the purity of the doctrine and canon, the treatises and teachings of Buddhism were open to revision.

The problem of deciding which works and teachings were authentic was compounded by the fact that Śākyamuni left no clear instructions concerning how spurious texts were to be identified. This left the door open for new texts and doctrines and created innumerable difficulties in

7 See Lewis Lancaster's "The Oldest Mahāyāna Sūtra: Its Significance for the Study of Buddhist Development," which points out some changes in the dated Chinese versions of the *Sūtra on the Perfection of Wisdom in Eight Thousand Lines* (*The Eastern Buddhist* 8.1 [1975], pp. 30–41).

interpretation and practice; but on the positive side it allowed the Buddhist canon to remain fluid. Because of this, the body of authoritative writings was able to adapt and grow, incorporating religious insights from many quarters.

Perhaps the most historically and doctrinally significant development in the centuries following Śākyamuni's death was the movement that came to be known as "Mahāyāna" (Tib. *theg pa chen po*), a term that literally means "Great Vehicle." The origins of this movement are obscure, and contemporary scholars have advanced a number of theories concerning when, where, and by whom it was developed.[8] It appears to have begun as an unorganized movement centered in local cults, each with its own texts and practices. Distinctively Mahāyāna works apparently began to appear during the first or second centuries C.E., several hundred years after the death of Śākyamuni. Some of these were referred to as "*sūtra*s," implying that they had been spoken by the Buddha, even though he had been dead for centuries.[9]

This discrepancy was noted by early Mahāyānists, who explained that Śākyamuni gave these teachings to a select few followers during his lifetime

8 There are a number of plausible explanations for the origins of Mahāyāna. One popular view holds that it was a movement of lay Buddhists who resented the exalted status and spiritual perquisites of the monks and who developed a more inclusive form of Buddhism that could include the aspirations of laypeople. This is the thesis argued by Étienne Lamotte (see, for instance, his article, "Mahāyāna Buddhism," in Heinz Bechert and Richard Gombrich, eds., *The World of Buddhism* [London: Thames & Hudson, 1984], pp. 90–93) and Akira Hirakawa ("The Rise of Mahāyāna Buddhism and Its Relationship to the Worship of Stūpas," *Memoirs of the Research Department of the Toyo Bunko* 22 [1963], pp. 57–106). This view is widely held among Japanese scholars, who tend to emphasize the role of the laity in Mahāyāna. Other scholars see the origins of Mahāyāna in devotional cults centered on the veneration of *stūpas*. Another view is advanced by Gregory Schopen ("The Phrase '*sa pṛthivīpradeśaś caityabhūto bhavet*' in the *Vajracchedikā*: Notes on the Cult of the Book in Mahāyāna," *Indo-Iranian Journal* 17 [1975], pp. 147–181; and "Two Problems in the History of Indian Buddhism: The Layman/Monk Distinction and the Doctrines of the Transference of Merit," *Studien zur Indologie und Iranistik* 10 [1985], pp. 9–47), who contends that the earliest traceable Mahāyāna groups were centered on veneration and propagation of particular texts. I find Schopen's arguments to be very persuasive, but there is still a great deal of uncertainty about the early phases of Mahāyāna.

9 As Graeme MacQueen notes, however, these sūtras are so different in form and content from those found in the Pāli canon that they cannot possibly be attempts to forge new sūtras. Rather, their authors are clearly aware that their writings represent a decisive break with established tradition and that they are at the forefront of a new and revolutionary movement. See his "Inspired Speech in Early Mahāyāna Buddhism II," *Religion* 12 (1982), p. 51.

but that most of his disciples (referred to as "hearers") were unprepared for these advanced doctrines, and so the texts were hidden in the realm of *nāga*s (beings with serpentlike bodies and human heads who live under the water) until people appeared in the world who were able to understand and explain them. Early in the second century C.E., several qualified teachers were born, and the texts were returned to the world of humans. The most important of these was Nāgārjuna, generally credited with being the main expositor of the "Middle Way School" (*dBu ma, Madhyamaka*), which systematized the Mahāyāna teachings of emptiness (discussed below) and the path of the bodhisattva. Bodhisattvas are Buddhist practitioners who eschew the nirvana of arhats and resolve to attain buddhahood in order to benefit other beings.

The earliest dated version of a text that can be confidently associated with Mahāyāna is a Chinese translation of the *Perfection of Wisdom in Eight Thousand Lines* by Lokakṣema, in the second century C.E. Although some of the doctrines and practices that are commonly associated with Mahāyāna are absent in this text, other characteristically Mahāyāna concepts are expounded, particularly the ideal of the bodhisattva and the doctrine of emptiness. It should be noted that both of these terms (as well as many other important Mahāyāna concepts) are also found in non-Mahāyāna sources, but their treatment in Mahāyāna treatises is distinctive.

By the time Buddhism arrived in Tibet, Mahāyāna had become a well-defined religious movement that saw itself as separate from (and superior to) other forms of Buddhism. These it labeled as "Hīnayāna" (Tib. *theg pa dman pa*), which literally means "Lesser (or Inferior) Vehicle." The following sections will examine some of the main ideas and images of the Mahāyāna Buddhism that entered Tibet.

The Perfection of Wisdom Literature

The earliest clearly Mahāyāna texts are the "Perfection of Wisdom" sūtras, which were probably composed during the first and second centuries C.E. Although they hold many terms and doctrines in common with earlier schools of Buddhism, they represent a major paradigm shift in the tradition. According to Graeme MacQueen, "as is often the case with revolutionaries, many of the terminological and conceptual resources available to them were in the tradition with which they were breaking," but these terms were often used in strikingly new ways.[10]

In these texts, the ideal of personal liberation is denounced, and the figure of the bodhisattva is valorized. The Perfection of Wisdom sūtras also discourse at length on the doctrine of emptiness (*stong pa nyid, śūnyatā*), which holds that all phenomena are empty of inherent existence and are merely collections of parts that arise due to causes and conditions. Thus they utterly lack any essence. These truths are only fully understood by those who develop the "perfection of wisdom" (*shes rab kyi pha rol tu phyin pa, prajñā-pāramitā*), which allows sages to free themselves from the shackles of false conceptuality and perceive reality as it is. The true nature of reality is referred to in these texts as "suchness" (*de bzhin nyid, tathatā*), which is described as ineffable and utterly beyond the realm of language or conceptual thought. It is associated with emptiness and is only known by yogic adepts who transcend language and conceptuality. Such people enter into direct understanding of reality as it is, freed from the false imaginings of conceptually influenced consciousness.

Like the discourses contained in the Pāli canon, the Perfection of Wisdom sūtras generally begin with the standard opening line: "Thus have I heard at one time: the Bhagavan [Buddha] was dwelling in . . ." Many of the places where the discourses are situated are also mentioned in the Pāli texts, and Buddha's main disciples are often present (although in the Perfection of Wisdom texts they are commonly portrayed as being inferior in understanding to bodhisattvas).

There are many other divergences, and among the more notable ones are the changes in the way the Buddha is presented. In the Perfection of Wisdom literature he becomes a cosmic figure whose understanding surpasses that of all humans and gods, and his power allows him to transcend the ordinary laws of time and space. No longer a mortal human teacher, he generates bodies that pervade all of space, is omniscient (an attribute that Buddha denies in the Pāli canon), and, perhaps most strikingly, he declares that he never truly dies or enters a final nirvana. Rather, he only *appeared* to pass away for the benefit of his hearer disciples, who needed this graphic lesson in impermanence so that they would make greater effort in religious

10 Graeme MacQueen, "Inspired Speech in Early Mahāyāna Buddhism II," p. 61.

practice. Although they believed that Śākyamuni died and entered a final nirvana, he continues to live in a "pure land," where advanced practitioners still visit him and receive his teachings.

In addition to these doctrinal changes, the Perfection of Wisdom sūtras differ stylistically from the Pāli discourses. For one thing, many of them are much longer than the Pāli texts, and the dialogue is strikingly different in tone and content.[11] Another change occurs in the cast of characters: in many of these texts bodhisattvas appear as interlocutors and teachers, and they are portrayed as vastly superior in understanding to the Hīnayānists. Perhaps the most striking change in these texts is found in the content of the discourses. In the Pāli texts Buddha presents his teachings as accurate descriptions of the true nature of reality, but in the Perfection of Wisdom literature the ultimate validity of these presentations is denied. Buddha tells his audience that his doctrines are mere words that only operate on the level of conceptuality. This is even true of the goals of the path, and he informs them that there is no truly existent nirvana, and no truly existent person who attains it. Thus in the *Diamond Sūtra* Buddha tells Subhūti,

> due to being established in the bodhisattva vehicle, one should give rise to the thought, "As many sentient beings there are that are included among the realms of sentient beings . . . whatever realms of sentient beings can be conceived, all these should be brought by me to nirvana, to a final nirvana that is a realm of nirvana without remainder; but, although countless sentient beings have reached final nirvana, no sentient being whatsoever has reached final nirvana." Why is this? Subhūti, if a discrimination of a sentient being arises in a bodhisattva, he should not be called a bodhisattva. Why is this? Subhūti, one who gives rise to the discrimination of such a self, the discrimination of a sentient being, the discrimination of a soul, or the discrimination of a person should not be called a bodhisattva.[12]

11 The Perfection of Wisdom texts are often grouped according to length, and the longer ones may be elaborations of earlier versions. There also seems to have been a corresponding move toward brevity, and some later texts appear to be condensations of earlier versions.

12 Edward Conze, ed., *Vajracchedikāprajñāpāramitāsūtra* (Rome: Istituto Italiano per il Medio ed Estremo Oriente [1974]), pp. 29–32.

Even the term "bodhisattva" is merely a verbal designation lacking ultimate validity. Buddha's teachings are likewise mere words that at best indicate the direction of awakening but do not describe reality as it truly is; this can only be understood by those who transcend words and concepts.

Mahāyāna Doctrines

The Bodhisattva

The figure of the bodhisattva is central to Mahāyāna. The Sanskrit term literally means "awakening (*bodhi*) being (*sattva*)," and it indicates that a bodhisattva is someone who is progressing toward the state of awakening of a buddha. The term was translated into Tibetan as *byang chub sems dpa'*, which means "awakening hero," indicating that the bodhisattva is viewed by Tibetans as a noble and courageous figure. This reflects the fact that bodhisattvas are often depicted in Mahāyāna literature as mythic heroes, possessing supernatural powers and ceaselessly working for the benefit of others.

The bodhisattva is commonly contrasted with the Hīnayāna ideal of the arhat, who seeks to escape from cyclic existence but is primarily concerned with personal liberation. The bodhisattva, by contrast, seeks to establish all sentient beings in awakening and even takes on their karmic burdens. Mahāyāna texts indicate that bodhisattvas are able to transfer the sufferings and afflictions of others to themselves and that they also give their own merit to others.

The purview of the bodhisattva's compassion is universal, since bodhisattvas seek the liberation of all beings, without exception and without distinctions. It is admitted in Mahāyāna literature that arhats also have compassion and that they teach others. Moreover, the accomplishments of arhats are impressive: they overcome the afflictive emotions and eliminate hatred, ignorance, and desire for the things of cyclic existence. They become dispassionate toward material possessions, care nothing for worldly fame and power, and because of this they transcend the mundane world. When they die, they pass beyond the world into a blissful state of nirvana in which there is no further rebirth and no suffering. Despite these attainments, however, their path is denigrated by the Mahāyāna sūtras, which draw a sharp distinction between the "great compassion" of bodhisattvas and the limited compassion of arhats.

Hīnayāna is divided by Mahāyāna exegetes into two paths: the path of "hearers" (*nyan thos, śrāvaka*) and the path of "solitary realizers" (*rang sangs rgyas, pratyeka-buddha*). The term "hearers" originally referred to the immediate disciples of Śākyamuni, who heard his words and practiced meditation in accordance with the literal meaning of his instructions. According to Mahāyānists, they believed that the teachings they heard were the only ones taught by Śākyamuni and that all other doctrines attributed to him (including Mahāyāna discourses) are spurious. Mahāyānists further contend that Śākyamuni propounded doctrines that surpassed his Hīnayāna teachings, but hearers were not permitted to listen to them because their cognitive capacities were inferior to those for whom he presented his Mahāyāna lectures. Although they criticize Hīnayāna on these grounds, Mahāyānists also contend that Hīnayāna paths are valid ways of making spiritual progress and that they were taught for certain people who are primarily interested in personal liberation and not in working for the salvation of others.

Solitary realizers are Hīnayāna practitioners who attain liberation by themselves, without hearing the teachings of a buddha. According to Mahāyāna explanations, they previously listened to buddhas and followed their teachings, but in their final lives they have no teachers. Seeking only personal salvation, they attain nirvana as quickly as possible and pass beyond cyclic existence.

Many Mahāyāna texts adopt a strongly sectarian tone when discussing Hīnayānists. This attitude is also found in Tibetan presentations of the differences between Hīnayāna and Mahāyāna, despite the fact that from the earliest period of Buddhism's dissemination into Tibet Mahāyāna has been the dominant tradition. Although there is little evidence of proselytizing by Hīnayānists in Tibet, Buddhists in the Land of Snows adopted the tone of their Indian teachers in their discussions of Hīnayāna.

Why Mahāyāna Is Superior

According to the Dalai Lama, Mahāyāna is superior to Hīnayāna in three ways: (1) motivation, (2) goal, and (3) level of understanding.[13] Mahāyāna

13 Tenzin Gyatso, H.H. the Fourteenth Dalai Lama, in *Tantra in Tibet: The Great Exposition of Secret Mantra by Tsong-ka-pa, Part One* (London: Allen & Unwin, 1977), pp. 91–104.

surpasses Hīnayāna in terms of motivation in that bodhisattvas are inspired by great compassion—which encompasses all sentient beings—while Hīnayānists only seek liberation for themselves. The bodhisattva's goal of buddhahood is superior to the arhat's intention to attain a personal nirvana, since it takes much longer to reach and requires perfection of compassion and wisdom, along with innumerable good qualities, whereas the arhat only needs to eliminate the coarser levels of the afflictions and develop complete dispassion toward cyclic existence, along with a direct perception of emptiness. Although the Dalai Lama states that arhats do understand emptiness (since without this they would be unable to pass beyond cyclic existence), he contends that a buddha's understanding of emptiness is infinitely more profound.

In addition to these criticisms, Mahāyānists also assert that their vehicle is superior to that of their opponents because it is able to encompass more people and bring them to awakening. They characterize Hīnayāna as a narrow, limited path suitable only for monks, but Mahāyāna is portrayed as a comprehensive tradition with room for everyone. It has teachings and practices for lay people as well as monks, and Mahāyāna texts stress the importance of the ability to adapt the doctrine to the individual needs and proclivities of one's audience.

The Bodhisattva Path

The career of a bodhisattva begins with the first dawning of the "mind of awakening" (*byang chub kyi sems, bodhicitta*), which represents a fundamental alteration in one's attitudes. Ordinary beings—even those who are kind and compassionate—are primarily motivated by self-interest and work mainly for their own benefit. All of their activities and thoughts are tinged by self-serving motivations and attitudes. Even when they perform acts of kindness, they generally do so expecting praise or personal satisfaction and not because of pure altruism.

Bodhisattvas, however, are motivated by universal compassion, and they seek the ultimate goal of buddhahood in order to be of service to others. They embark on this path with the generation of the mind of awakening. Unlike ordinary beings, who think of their own advantage, bodhisattvas consider how best to benefit others.

Differences between Arhats and Bodhisattvas according to Mahāyāna

	Arhats	Bodhisattvas
Motivation	Liberation for themselves	Compassion for all beings
Goal	Personal nirvana	Liberation of all sentient beings
Level of understanding	1. Direct perception of emptiness	1. Omniscience
	2. Supernatural abilities such as clairvoyance, knowledge of past lives	2. Full comprehension of emptiness
Qualities attained	1. Eliminate coarse levels of afflictions	1. Six (or ten) perfections (generosity, ethics, patience, effort, concentration, wisdom)
	2. Dispassion toward cyclic existence	2. Great compassion
	3. Ability to levitate up to the level of seven śāla trees	3. Skill in means
		4. Full comprehension of emptiness in all its aspects at all times
		5. Supernatural abilities such as transcendence of time and laws of physics
Length of training period	Three human lifetimes	Minimum of three countless eons from manifestation of mind of awakening

Bodhisattvas are deeply moved by the torments of sentient beings, and they do whatever they can to help them. At the beginning of the bodhisattva path, they realize that at present their powers are limited and that they are unable even to prevent their own sufferings. In order to improve their ability to aid sentient beings in distress, bodhisattvas resolve to become buddhas, since buddhas have the greatest possible capacity to help others. Buddhas possess unlimited wisdom and compassion, and they have perfected the ability to adapt their instructions to suit the needs of individuals.

The Six Perfections

After generating the mind of awakening, a bodhisattva begins a training program intended to culminate in the attainment of buddhahood. Along the way, he or she will develop innumerable good qualities, the most important of which are the six "perfections" (*pha rol tu phyin pa, pāramitā*): (1) generosity, (2) ethics, (3) patience, (4) effort, (5) concentration, and (6) wisdom. These constitute the core of the awakened personality of a buddha. This list is often supplemented with an additional list of four perfections: (7) skill in means, (8) aspiration, (9) power, and (10) exalted wisdom. These ten are correlated in some Mahāyāna texts with the ten bodhisattva levels, which are stages of progress beginning with the mind of awakening and culminating in buddhahood.

1. *The Perfection of Generosity.* The first perfection involves overcoming selfishness and attachment to material things and a corresponding attitude of willingness to give everything one has to others. Those who have perfected this quality are willing even to donate parts of their bodies to those in need. On a more mundane level, bodhisattvas develop a disposition toward freely giving away all of their possessions, without feeling any sense of loss and without expecting any recompense or praise.

   Bodhisattvas sometimes give away material objects, and they also help others by sharing Buddhist teachings. The latter is by far the more valuable gift, since beings caught up in cyclic existence only benefit temporarily when given money or possessions. Such things inevitably are lost, the relief that they bring is only temporary, and acquiring them may have the negative side-effect of deepening attachment. Teaching sentient beings about the Buddhist path is more worthwhile, because through following it they will eventually transcend all suffering.
2. *The Perfection of Ethics.* The second perfection is a basic prerequisite for the Mahāyāna path. In cultivating this quality, bodhisattvas first discipline themselves to avoid physical expressions of afflicted thoughts, the negative actions that result in future suffering. Next they must work at eliminating even the predispositions toward such actions. This process has a number of important results, including mental equanimity and bet-

ter rebirths.[14] A person who avoids negative actions and engages in ethical behavior will enjoy concordant benefits in the future, but the development of mental calm is equally essential. The minds of ordinary beings are agitated by afflicted thoughts, which lead to negative actions, and these in turn result in suffering and a tendency to engage in similar actions in the future. Training in ethics serves to calm the mind, to diminish the force of afflictive emotions, and thus provides an important precondition to advanced meditative training, which requires mental stability.

3. *The Perfection of Patience.* The third perfection involves developing an attitude of unshakable equanimity. This is important because anger can destroy the good qualities one has cultivated and eliminate hard-won equanimity.

   The bodhisattva understands that all phenomena arise in dependence on causes and conditions and lack any essence. Beings who bring harm to others are part of this causal network and are neither evil nor good in themselves. They are reacting to external and internal stimuli and are guided by their own past actions and present attitudes. Thus the bodhisattva realizes that it makes no more sense to hate a person who harms one than it would to hold a branch personally responsible for falling on one's head.

4. *The Perfection of Effort.* Because of the difficulties bodhisattvas encounter and the length of time required to complete their training, they need to maintain continued enthusiasm for the path. Since it may require eons to complete, it is necessary to cultivate an attitude of sustained fervor. The bodhisattva's determination is strengthened by compassion for others: she wishes to be able to help them alleviate their sufferings, and since buddhas are best able to accomplish this, she works tirelessly toward this goal.

5. *The Perfection of Concentration.* After developing an attitude of altruism and nonattachment toward material things, cultivating a calm mind that is spontaneously ethical and patient, and generating an unflagging determination to work toward awakening for the benefit of others, the

14 According to Buddhism, the favorable rebirths are those of humans, demigods, and gods. Negative rebirths are those of animals, hungry ghosts, and hell beings. The former group enjoys greater freedom from suffering, while the lives of beings in the latter group are painful and are the result of negative karma.

bodhisattva is prepared for the perfection of concentration. This involves cultivating the ability to focus one-pointedly on an object of observation, without being disturbed by mental wavering.

6. *The Perfection of Wisdom.* The perfection of wisdom is often declared in Mahāyāna texts to be the culmination of all the others. Bodhisattvas who actualize it are able to see things as they really are, freed from false conceptuality. One who perfects wisdom understands that all phenomena are empty of inherent existence, created by causes and conditions external to themselves, and that they are collections of parts lacking any essence.

   This realization is essential because sentient beings transmigrate powerlessly due to misperceiving the nature of phenomena. They view things as naturally possessing the qualities imputed to them by conceptual thought and as truly desirable, detestable, etc. The result of such thinking is desire, hatred, and other afflictive emotions, which are only overcome by one who recognizes that all phenomena utterly lack inherent existence and are mere collections of constantly changing parts, which are moved along by causes and conditions.

   The recognition of all phenomena as empty does not, however, diminish the bodhisattva's compassion. Sentient beings are recognized as impermanent collections of changing parts, and the bodhisattva understands that their present sufferings are the results of past misdeeds. Perceiving them as psycho-physical continuums whose future will be influenced by present actions and attitudes, the bodhisattva works to help them to change in ways that are conducive to future happiness.

Buddhahood

The culmination of the bodhisattva's training is the attainment of buddhahood. At this point, all afflictions have been overcome, and the natural luminosity of the mind shines forth. There is no longer even a desire to work for the benefit of others, but due to cultivating compassion in limitless ways for an unimaginable period of time, the buddha continues spontaneously to manifest compassion. The buddha's mind has attained a level of total omniscience, unhindered by any obstructions or limitations. This omniscience fully comprehends all realms, things, aspects, and times.

In addition, the buddha manifests three bodies: (1) the truth body (*chos kyi sku, dharma-kāya*); (2) the complete enjoyment body (*longs spyod pa'i sku, saṃbhoga-kāya*); and (3) emanation bodies (*sprul sku, nirmāṇa-kāya*). The first is divided into two aspects: the wisdom truth body (*ye shes chos sku, jñāna-dharma-kāya*) and the nature truth body (*ngo bo nyid chos sku, svabhāvika-dharma-kāya*). The first refers to a buddha's omniscient consciousness, and the second is the emptiness of that consciousness. The complete enjoyment body is a pure form (said in Tibetan Buddhism to be produced from subtle energies called "winds" in conjunction with consciousness), which resides in a pure land. Emanation bodies are physical manifestations that buddhas create in order to benefit sentient beings.

3: Some Important Buddhist Doctrines

Karma and Rebirth

As we have seen, after the Buddha's passing numerous schools arose, and new discourses appeared that propounded doctrines and practices not present in earlier canons (and in some cases new interpretations). There is a great deal of discussion among scholars concerning what the Buddha actually taught and which doctrines can legitimately be ascribed to him. Although many of the discourses that are accepted by Tibetans as being the words of Śākyamuni Buddha are of doubtful historical authenticity, there is, nevertheless, little debate within the tradition that their source is in fact the Buddha. Thus, for the purposes of the present study the focus will be on what Tibetans believe the Buddha taught and not on what modern historians would accept as authentic teachings.

Among the most basic and pervasive of these are teachings attributed to the Buddha concerning karma and rebirth. These ideas were already present in the culture in which he was born, and he accepted them in much the same way that his contemporaries did. According to Tibetan Buddhists, the Buddha taught that one's present life is only one in a beginningless series of incarnations, and each of these is determined by one's actions in previous lives. These actions are collectively referred to as "karma." This idea specifically refers to one's volitional actions, which may be good, bad, or neutral. Actions give rise to corresponding effects: good, bad, and neutral experiences are the direct results of good, bad, and neutral karma. This is presented as a universal law that has nothing to do with abstract ideas of justice, reward, or punishment. It does not require the control, intervention, or modification of any outside power; as long as one remains within cyclic existence one performs actions, and these inevitably produce concordant results.

If one fails to recognize the causally interconnected nature of karma and rebirth, one will continue to transmigrate helplessly in cyclic existence. As we have seen in the life of the Buddha, however, it is possible to break the vicious cycle and escape from the sufferings that repeated births bring. The cycle is driven by ignorance, and the key to liberation lies in overcoming ignorance. The Buddha is the paradigm of a person who has accomplished this, and so devout Buddhists strive to emulate his example. The first requirement is the development of dissatisfaction with cyclic existence. As long as one is basically comfortable within the cycle of rebirth, there is no possibility of release. One must develop a profound revulsion, looking back on one's beginningless lives with disgust and vowing to break the pattern by any means necessary.

Next, one must emulate the Buddha's example and develop the positive moral qualities that he cultivated. This leads to mental peace and equanimity, which are necessary for successful meditation. Meditation is the key to overcoming ignorance, for through mental training one can develop insight into the true nature of reality, which acts as a counteragent to ignorance. Successful attainment of insight allows one to transcend the influence of karma, to end ignorant engagement in actions that bind one to continued transmigration, and eventually to end the cycle altogether.

Appearance and Reality

According to Buddhist meditation theory, the basic causes of suffering are cognitive in origin. We mentally create a vision of reality, but because of ignorance this vision is skewed and does not reflect things as they are. Some of our wrong ideas are harmless, but others lead to the creation of negative mental states, such as ignorance, desire, or hatred. One of the most dangerous of these mistaken concepts is the false notion of a self, which Buddhist meditation theory contends is innately present in all human beings. On a very basic level, every person believes in a self or soul that is uncreated, immortal, unchanging, and permanent. Contrary to some other religious systems, Buddhism denies the existence of such an entity and contends that in order to attain liberation one must eliminate the false belief in a self or soul.

There has been some disagreement among Western scholars of Buddhism concerning whether or not Śākyamuni Buddha really advocated this idea, but there is no debate among Tibetan scholars, who view the concept of no-self (*bdag med, anātman*) as a cornerstone of Buddhist thought and practice. In Tibetan meditation texts, belief in a self or soul is said to be based on a false imputation, and techniques to examine this notion in order to eradicate it are an important focus of meditation literature.

But if the concept is common to all human beings, where do we get it? And if it is mistaken, why is it so universally accepted? The answer, Buddhist texts suggest, is that although there is a basis for belief in a self the imputation is still a false one. The basis for the imputation of self is the collection of elements that together constitute the psycho-physical personality, which Buddhism divides into five "aggregates" (*phung po, skandha*): (1) form, (2) feelings, (3) discriminations, (4) compositional factors, and (5) consciousness.

These are the constituents of all impermanent phenomena and are the basis on which we impute the notions of "I" and "mine." Taken together, they are the components of the individual, but we mistakenly impute something more: an essence, a self or soul. When one analyzes this concept to locate its basis, however, all one finds are these five factors, none of which can constitute a self because they are constantly changing, whereas the self that sentient beings imagine is self-sufficient and enduring.

Form refers to phenomena that comprise the physical world, which includes the sense organs (eye, ear, nose, tongue, body, and mind) and their objects. *Feelings* are our sensations of things, and these are divided into three types: pleasant, unpleasant, and neutral. They result when the senses come into contact with objects. *Discriminations* are the differentiations we make regarding objects of perception as a result of contact. They cause us to discriminate between colors, sounds, smells, tastes, tangible objects, and mental images. *Consciousness* includes the six types of consciousnesses: eye, ear, nose, tongue, body, and mind. *Compositional factors* are volitional activities, both good and bad. Karma is included within compositional factors, since it directs the mind in particular directions, thus influencing the content of future mental states.

Taken together, these five aggregates constitute the psycho-physical personality, and Buddhist teachers claim that the totality of an individual is included within this group. Ordinary beings, however, superimpose an enduring, uncreated "self" that exists apart from and independently of these constituents, but this is nothing more than a label applied to what are really constantly changing phenomena. This mistaken notion leads to grasping and attachment, which in turn result in harmful actions, and so the mistaken belief in a self is said to be one of the most powerful factors that keep ordinary beings enmeshed in cyclic existence.

The false conception of self is deeply ingrained, and every sentient being has cultivated it not only in the present lifetime but for countless past lives. Since it has been reified and strengthened over such a long period, it is deeply embedded in our basic assumptions and consequently very difficult to dislodge. Because of its strength, it is not possible to eradicate the idea of self all at once through simply recognizing that the belief is untenable (although this is an important first step). One initially understands no-self conceptually, through a process of reasoning. The reasoning begins with a consideration of how the self appears to us—that is, as something that is autonomous, enduring, and independent of the psycho-physical continuum.

The meditator should consider whether or not the self can exist in the way that it appears. He first determines that if there is a self, it must be either separate from or identical with the psycho-physical aggregates. If it is different from them, then there is no connection between the self and the meditator, since they are different factualities. The self appears to consciousness as something enduring and autonomous, but all of us are impermanent and only exist due to causes and conditions that are external to ourselves. The only constant in human life is change, and all the constituents of the psycho-physical personality are changing from moment to moment; thus the meditator should conclude that even if there were a self different from the aggregates, it would be unrelated to him, since an autonomous, enduring entity could have no conceivable relation with an impermanent being.

Having eliminated the possibility of a self that exists independently of the aggregates, one then considers the possibility that there might be a self which is the same as the aggregates. If there is such a self, it must be the same as at least one of them; but when one examines each in turn one realizes that they are all impermanent, changing from moment to moment, and there is no underlying unity or essence that remains throughout the ongoing process of change.

The only conclusion that can legitimately be reached is that the self is a fiction, a mere label superimposed onto the aggregates, a concept created and reified by the mind but lacking any substantial reality. This reasoning process alone does not eliminate the idea, however; it merely weakens it. Because it is so deeply ingrained, the idea of self is only eliminated through repeated meditation on the reasonings of no-self, which enable the yogin to become progressively more familiar with the understanding that no self or essence exists. The Dalai Lama concludes that "when such a realization is maintained and reinforced through constant meditation and familiarization, you will be able to develop it into an intuitive or direct experience."[15]

Many Westerners reject this notion, contending that it would be a sort of cognitive suicide. The idea that the self (which is assumed even by people who reject religions that propound the idea) does not exist is profoundly disturbing to many non-Buddhists, but in Buddhist thought the denial of self is not seen as constituting a loss, but rather is viewed as a profoundly liberating insight. Since the innate idea of self implies an autonomous, unchanging essence, if such a thing were in fact the core of one's being, it would mean that change would be impossible, and one would be stuck being just what one is right now. Because there is no such self, however, we are open toward the future. One's nature is never fixed and determined, and so through engaging in Buddhist practice one can exert control over the process of change and progress in wisdom, compassion, patience, and other good qualities. One can even become a buddha, a fully awakened being who is completely liberated from all the frailties, sufferings, and limitations of ordinary beings. But this is only possible because there is no permanent and static self, no soul that exists self-sufficiently, separated from the ongoing process of change.

Such intellectual understanding is not enough by itself, however. Even when beginning meditators gain a conceptual grasp of the doctrine of emptiness, it does not weaken the strength of the appearances of inherent existence. People and things still appear to exist from their own side,

15 Tenzin Gyatso, H.H. the Fourteenth Dalai Lama, *Path to Bliss* (Ithaca: Snow Lion Publications, 1991), p. 201.

independently of external causes and conditions. On a personal level, even when one intellectually recognizes that there is no basis for the mistaken concept of "I," this false idea still appears. As an analogy, a physicist might know that the table in front of her is mostly composed of space and that the matter of the table consists of infinitesimally tiny particles in a constant state of vibration, but the table still appears as a solid, hard object.

Because intellectual comprehension of a concept is not the same as fully grasping it, Buddhist texts make a distinction between three levels of understanding, which are called respectively "wisdom arisen from hearing," "wisdom arisen from thinking," and "wisdom arisen from meditating." The first type is the superficial understanding one gains from simply hearing someone else teaching something. It does not involve a great deal of analysis, but is primarily based on listening to someone and comprehending the meaning of the words. Wisdom arisen from thinking comes from pondering the significance of what one has heard and gaining a deeper understanding, although this is still only conceptual. Wisdom arisen from meditating dawns when one fully internalizes what one has learned and pondered, through apprehending it with direct perception on a level that transcends merely conceptual realization. At this level of awareness, one moves beyond dependence on the mere words of the teaching and perceives the truth directly.

Dependent Arising

Closely connected with the idea of no-self is the doctrine of dependent arising (*rten cing 'brel bar 'byung ba, pratītya-samutpāda*), which holds that all compounded phenomena arise due to causes and conditions external to themselves, remain in existence due to causes and conditions, and eventually pass away due to other causes and conditions. This process is broken down into twelve steps, which are referred to as the "twelve links of dependent arising":

(1) ignorance
(2) action
(3) consciousness
(4) name and form
(5) the six sources

(6) contact
(7) feeling
(8) attachment
(9) grasping
(10) existence
(11) birth
(12) aging and death

In this process, the primary factor is *ignorance*. This is not just an absence of knowledge but is also a consciousness that perceives reality incorrectly. It motivates beings to engage in actions, but since the basis of the actions is mistaken, they lead to negative reactions. The most basic type of ignorance is the belief in an inherently existent self, which gives rise to thoughts of acquiring things for this self to possess.

In the context of the schema of the twelve links of dependent arising, *action* generally refers to a defining act that determines one's future rebirth. If this deed is meritorious, one will be reborn in one of the three good transmigrations—human, demigod, or god. If it is a negative action, one will be reborn in one of the three lower transmigrations—animal, hungry ghost, or hell being.[16]

The defining action conditions one's *consciousness*, since each type of transmigration has a distinctive type of mind. (All are characterized by basic ignorance, however, and ignorant thoughts tend to perpetuate themselves.) At the beginning of a new life, one acquires a particular sort of cognition, and this is determined by one's past deeds. If one is born as a human, one will have a human consciousness, which will be conditioned by previous moral decisions and actions. Moreover, a human who engaged in acts of violence in a past life, for instance, will be predisposed toward violence in the present life, and unless he does something to reverse this trend, he will likely

16 Demigods (*asura*) are beings with greater power than humans but who are inferior to gods (*deva*). Their inferior status makes them intensely jealous, and so they wage war against the gods, even though they are doomed to lose. Hungry ghosts (*preta*) are beings with enormous stomachs and tiny throats who are constantly pained by hunger and thirst. When they find food or water, however, it appears to be a disgusting substance like pus or blood. They are never satisfied and are born in this situation due to being greedy and avaricious in their past lives. Hell beings are at the lowest level of cyclic existence; they reside in various infernal realms in which they suffer terrible torments as a result of their past negative actions.

repeat the pattern in the present life, leading to negative karma and a lower rebirth.

Consciousness conditions the next link, *name and form*. *Name* refers to the aggregates of feelings, discriminations, compositional factors, and consciousness. *Form* refers to the aggregate of form. Together these constitute the psycho-physical personality, and this is conditioned by the predispositions that have been inherited from past lives.

The *six sources* are the sense powers of eye, ear, nose, tongue, body, and mind. As the form aggregate develops, these also mature, and the process is influenced by the previous four members. As the sense powers operate, one begins to have contact with external things, and this contact is also conditioned by the previous stages. *Contact* is the coming together of object, sense faculty, and consciousness. It conditions the next link, *feeling*, which has the function of discriminating some things as pleasant, some as unpleasant, and others as neutral in accordance with how they are distinguished in contact.

All of these are conditioned by ignorance, and so they are all mistaken with respect to their appearing objects. As one develops ideas of pleasure, pain, and neutrality, one begins to grasp at things that are pleasant and avoid things that are unpleasant. Thus one experiences *grasping* and *attachment*, the eighth and ninth links of the process.

These in turn create the basis for continued *existence*. Existence results from grasping and attachment: when one becomes attracted to the things of cyclic existence, one assures that in the future one will again be reborn. This is a predisposition that began with ignorance, which in turn prompted actions, and these led to contact and grasping.

All of these taken together constitute the link to future *birth*. Due to the force of previously generated desires, a being who is about to be reborn feels desire toward its future parents. If the being is to be reborn as a male, it will feel desire toward its future mother, and if it will be a female, it will feel desire toward its future father. Moreover, the type of being toward which it will be attracted is determined by the nature of its past karma. If its karma destines it for rebirth as a human, then it will be drawn toward human parents, and if it will be reborn as an animal, then it will seek out animal parents, and so forth. It will be attracted to a male and female who are about to copulate and who are appropriate for its future life situation. The completion of the process of rebirth occurs when the future father impregnates the future mother, and the being takes rebirth in the appropriate life situation. The moment of physical birth is the culmination of this process.

The final factor, *aging and death*, begins at the moment of birth. Everything that is born is moving toward death, and in each moment cells are dying and being replaced by new ones. Eventually the regeneration process begins to break down, and one's physical condition degenerates. The inevitable result is death.

Most beings are beguiled by the transitory things of cyclic existence and seek to acquire those that are perceived as pleasant. They are blind to the inevitable results of such actions, which only bind them to continued rebirth and resultant sufferings. As we will see in the next section, the cycle can be broken, but it requires a profound restructuring of cognition through meditation.

4: Meditation

The Role of Meditation in Indian and Tibetan Buddhism

Tibetan Buddhism has many different schools and lineages, with a variety of practices and goals. All schools of Tibetan Buddhism agree, however, that the final goal of Mahāyāna practice is the attainment of buddhahood for the benefit of all other sentient beings. The key factor in this process is meditation (*bsgom pa, bhāvanā*), a general term that encompasses a wide range of practices and goals. Some of these aim at pacifying the mind and quieting the mental confusion that afflicts ordinary beings. Other meditative practices are concerned with developing clear understanding of Buddhist tenets such as the four noble truths, impermanence, no-self, etc., or with cultivating direct perception of the true nature of reality.

According to the Dalai Lama, "meditation is a *familiarization* of the mind with an object of meditation."[17] Sentient beings have lived since beginningless time, and in every lifetime we have accustomed ourselves to wrong ideas, which has led to suffering, death, and rebirth. Since this preconditioning is deeply ingrained, the meditational process used to break its power requires a great deal of effort and repeated familiarization of the mind with meditational objects—Buddhist concepts, doctrines, symbols (and sometimes objects or images with no Buddhist associations).

Most meditative practices aim at some form of cognitive restructuring.

17 H.H. the Fourteenth Dalai Lama, *Kindness, Clarity, and Insight*, tr. Jeffrey Hopkins (Ithaca: Snow Lion Publications, 1984), p. 183.

Since dissatisfaction arises from wrong ideas, the solution to the problem of suffering lies in changing these ideas, and this is accomplished through meditation. Suffering is linked to actions based on afflictive mental states such as desire, ignorance, hatred, etc., and many of the techniques of Tibetan meditation are designed to serve as counteragents to afflictions. For instance, a meditator who is particularly prone to anger might be instructed by a meditation teacher to cultivate feelings of love and compassion. Love and compassion are incompatible with anger, and so the more one trains in the former attitudes, the more one's tendency toward anger diminishes.

A person with strong desire might be instructed to consider the impermanence of all the phenomena of cyclic existence. No matter how much money or power one accumulates, one must eventually lose them, either sooner or later. Even the richest people cannot know with certainty that they will still have their money in a week, a month, or a year. And no amount of wealth can forestall death, which is the final end of the ambitions, desires, and concerns of this present life. Through contemplating these truths, one should experience a diminution of mundane desires and a corresponding interest in pursuing religious practice, which can lead to ultimate and lasting happiness.

Meditation on Death

In many cases, Buddhist meditators contemplate the basic realities of cyclic existence—such as suffering, impermanence, and death—but at other times meditators purposely visualize things that are not real but which have a therapeutic purpose. For example, practitioners with strong sexual desire will sometimes mentally imagine the whole world filled with skeletons. This serves to remind them that all living things inevitably die, and so there is no good reason to be attached to any of them or to seek one's happiness in sexual activity. Alternatively, meditators sometimes bring to mind people they find particularly attractive and then imagine what these people will look like as decaying corpses. They will picture the corpses in various stages of decomposition and will consider how repulsive corpses are to the living. This meditation is sometimes done in burial grounds or cemeteries, since such places are said to be conducive to contemplation of death.

The outcome of this process should be a recognition that one's desire for particular individuals is only a result of deluded thinking, since there is nothing inherently attractive about anyone. If a particular person were inherently desirable, then he or she should be attractive to anyone at any time in any circumstance. That this is not the case is indicated by the fact that different societies (and different individuals) have varying standards of beauty: some consider thin bodies to be beautiful, while others view full figures as more appealing; some value light skin, while others prefer dark skin. Standards of shape and size of facial features vary between cultures, as do notions of ideal hair color and style. This variety indicates that there is no universal standard of beauty and that one's ideas of physical attractiveness are largely a result of conditioning.

In addition, if a particular person's body were inherently attractive, then it should still be attractive as a decaying corpse. The fact that images of corpses induce feelings of revulsion and horror indicates that beauty is a transient and conditioned thing. If one considers these factors, one should conclude that there is no good reason to desire any one person more than others. Beauty is in the eye (and mind) of the beholder, and through changing one's attitudes it is possible to overcome afflicted attachment. This does not mean that one should go through life viewing people as decaying corpses and feeling disgust toward them; the purpose of the meditation is to develop an attitude of equanimity. Excessive revulsion is as much an affliction as excessive desire. Since humans are particularly susceptible to desire, however, some need to cultivate rather extreme antidotes in order to counteract it.[18] It is unlikely that most people will be able to overcome sensual desire completely, but through repeated familiarization with these visualizations it is often possible to diminish its force. The end result of this meditation should be an outlook that views all living beings as equal and that realizes that feelings of attraction and revulsion are transient results of afflicted mental states.

18 In Indian and Tibetan Buddhism, the realm of existence that humans inhabit is called the Desire Realm because the predominant factor in this realm is desire. In the other two realms of existence, the Form Realm and the Formless Realm, desire does not afflict the inhabitants as much.

Stabilizing and Analytical Meditation

The minds of ordinary beings are scattered and confused, beguiled by surface appearances and deluded by false ideas. Advanced Buddhist meditators, by contrast, are said to have calm and disciplined minds, and they are able to see through appearances to understand the transient and unsatisfactory nature of the phenomena of cyclic existence.

Buddhist meditation literature contains many descriptions of meditative trainings that lead to equanimity and insight. An important goal of these practices is the attainment of "a union of calm abiding and higher insight," in which one is able to remain focused on a meditative object for as long as one wishes and at the same time to analyze its final nature.

In Mahāyāna literature, calm abiding and higher insight are often declared to be essential to advanced meditative practice. Calm abiding is so called because it is a state in which the mind remains fixed on an object of observation without wavering. It is characterized by the ability to fix one's attention on an internal object of observation for as long as one wishes, without being disturbed by mental fluctuation. According to Buddhist meditation literature, any object can be the basis for calm abiding, but meditators generally focus on objects that have soteriological value, such as the body of a buddha. Since one's ultimate goal is the attainment of buddhahood, this serves to orient the mind and purify mental obstructions.

The two primary obstacles to attainment of calm abiding are laxity (*bying ba, laya*) and excitement (*rgod pa, auddhatya*). The former is an internal dullness that diminishes mental clarity in meditative states. Excitement occurs when one's attention moves from object to object and one loses sight of the focal point of meditation.

Laxity and excitement diminish one's ability to concentrate, and so it is essential to overcome them. This is accomplished through development of mindfulness, a quality that allows the mind to examine itself and to recognize incipient laxity or excitement. When they appear, meditators apply antidotes to counteract them. When laxity arises or is about to arise, one counteracts it by brightening or enlarging the object of observation. Excitement may be counteracted in a number of ways: contemplating death and impermanence, decreasing the size and brightness of the object of observation, or heightened concentration on another object, such as the breath.

Physical and Mental Pliancy

During the training to develop calm abiding, meditators become progressively more adept at maintaining concentration. At the same time, the mind becomes agile and more perceptive. Just before attainment of fully developed calm abiding, the meditator has become so familiar with meditative concentration that all traces of physical lethargy and mental scattering have been eliminated. As a result, one experiences the arising of a factor of clarity referred to as "pliancy" (*shin tu sbyangs pa, praśrabdhi*). It is defined as "a serviceability of mind and body such that the mind can be set on a virtuous object of observation as long as one likes; it has the function of removing all obstructions."[19]

The four types of pliancy are: (1) mental pliancy, (2) physical pliancy, (3) bliss of physical pliancy, and (4) bliss of mental pliancy. Mental pliancy is a cognitive factor that removes "assumptions of bad states," which are subtle traces of nonvirtuous propensities that are the results of former negative actions and attitudes. Mental pliancy is experienced as a lightness of mind, and it is the result of successful cultivation of meditative stabilization.

A physical pliancy is "a special, light tangible object that removes physical tiredness and other unfavorable physical functionings."[20] Physical pliancies are the opposite of assumptions of bad states; they are physical factors generated by meditative stabilization.

With the arising of physical and mental pliancy, one also experiences a feeling of profound bliss, and one's body and mind feel light as wind. The bliss that accompanies the sense consciousnesses is referred to as "bliss of physical pliancy," and the bliss that is associated with mental consciousness is called "bliss of mental pliancy." These are connected with the removal of assumptions of bad states, which lead to heaviness of mind. According to Gendün Lodrö, due to the force of mental pliancy a subtle energy current called a "wind" courses through subtle channels in the body, giving rise to feelings of physical lightness, mental clarity, and great bliss.[21]

19 Jeffrey Hopkins, *Meditation on Emptiness* (London: Wisdom Publications, 1983), p. 252.

20 Geshe Gendün Lodrö, *Walking Through Walls*, tr. Jeffrey Hopkins (Ithaca: Snow Lion Publications, 1992), p. 205.

21 Ibid., p. 187.

Higher Insight

At this point one has overcome the assumptions of bad states, and one's mind and body are disciplined and serviceable. One has attained stability and equanimity due to pacifying the assumptions of bad states. As the initial euphoria of the bliss of mental pliancy fades, one's mind becomes fully pacified, and at this point one attains calm abiding, in which one maintains concentration without mental fluctuation; this is combined with mental pliancy.

Calm abiding is held to be a necessary prerequisite for attainment of higher insight, but meditators must initially cultivate stabilizing meditation and analytical meditation separately. When one has first developed calm abiding, one is not able to remain in that state while performing analysis, and so one must alternate between calming and analytical meditation. Through repeated practice, however, one develops the ability to maintain the two types of meditation in equal portions at the same time.

When this is accomplished, one turns one's analysis on the object of observation and considers its nature. One recognizes that it—like all phenomena of cyclic existence—is empty of inherent existence. All phenomena lack a self; they are dependently arisen due to the force of causes and conditions other than themselves. Through repeatedly familiarizing oneself with this notion, one gradually weakens the force of the appearance of inherent existence and directly apprehends the emptiness of the object of observation.

This, however, is not higher insight. Higher insight occurs when one's analytical meditation itself generates mental stability and is conjoined with physical and mental pliancy. At this point one enters into a powerful meditative stabilization that is characterized by stability and the appearance of a wisdom consciousness that understands the nature of the object of observation. The combination of stability and analysis in a single consciousness serves as a powerful counteragent to afflictions and is a potent tool for developing the ability to perceive emptiness directly.

The Five Buddhist Paths

Buddhist meditation texts distinguish five stages of spiritual advancement that constitute the path to awakening followed by meditators: (1) the path of accumulation, (2) the path of preparation, (3) the path of seeing, (4) the path of meditation, and (5) the path of no more learning.

The path of accumulation is so named because on this level one amasses the two "collections": the collection of merit and the collection of wisdom. The collection of merit consists of virtuous deeds and attitudes, which produce corresponding good karmic results and positive mental states. The collection of wisdom refers to cultivation of wisdom for the sake of all other sentient beings. One enters this path with the generation of the "mind of awakening."

The path of preparation is attained when a meditator reaches the level of a union of calm abiding and higher insight with emptiness as the object of observation. On this path, one gradually eliminates conceptuality in one's understanding of suchness (the true nature of reality, which is equated with emptiness).

During the path of preparation, meditators attain the highest worldly attributes and prepare to attain a supramundane path (the path of seeing). At this level, the cognizing subject no longer appears while one is in meditative stabilization. Prior to this, one had appearances of subject and object as distinct entities, but at the end of the path of preparation one is no longer able to ascertain subject or object. These factors do, however, still appear to the meditator, but she no longer consciously perceives them.

The meditator continues contemplating emptiness, and with repeated training all appearances of subject and object disappear in emptiness. All thoughts of subject and object are overcome, and one perceives emptiness directly. This marks the beginning of *the path of seeing*, and at this point subject and object are undifferentiable, like water poured into water.

On the path of seeing meditators remove the artificial conceptions of inherent existence, those which are acquired through training and studying mistaken philosophical systems. However, they do not yet remove the innate misconceptions of inherent existence, which are the results of conditioning since beginningless time and are more difficult to overcome.

Through repeated familiarization with emptiness, one is liberated from artificial innate conceptions with respect to the four noble truths and with respect to oneself, because one understands the emptiness of these concepts and of the consciousness that comprehends them.

Bodhisattvas on the path of seeing have transcended the condition of "ordinary beings" and have reached the state of "superiors" (*'phags pa, ārya*) because they have attained a supramundane path due to perceiving emptiness directly. Ordinary beings only view afflicted and false appearances and do not have direct perceptual awareness of emptiness. Mahāyānists on the path of seeing also enter the first of the ten "bodhisattva levels," called "the very joyous." These are progressive levels of attainment culminating in buddhahood.

During the path of seeing one removes the artificial or latent conceptions of inherent existence, but the subtler, innate traces of these conceptions remain and sometimes reassert themselves when one is not in meditative equipoise. During *the path of meditation* the subtlest traces are removed and will never reappear. This is because the mind is a clear and luminous entity, and when the adventitious conceptions of inherent existence are eliminated there is no longer any basis for their reemergence within one's mental continuum.

On the path of meditation, one continues to familiarize oneself with meditation on emptiness. The path of meditation is divided into uninterrupted paths and paths of liberation. On an uninterrupted path, meditators overcome innate conceptions of inherent existence, and the subsequent path of liberation is a meditative equipoise in which one is free from these cognitions. Meditators on the path of meditation also attain advanced meditative states that are neither uninterrupted paths nor paths of liberation. Bodhisattvas cultivate the remaining nine bodhisattva levels on the path of meditation.

The final phase of this process is *the path of no more learning*, during which meditators eliminate the very subtlest vestiges of the conception of inherent existence, together with its seeds. The culmination of the path of no more learning for Hīnayānists is the attainment of arhathood or the state of a solitary realizer, and for bodhisattvas it is the attainment of buddhahood. On the path of no more learning, bodhisattvas eliminate all the remaining traces of the afflictive obstructions and the obstructions to omniscience (the two primary sorts of afflictions that inhibit progress on the path) and reach their goal of attainment of buddhahood for the benefit of all living beings.

5: Tantra

The Place of the Tantras in Buddhist Literature

The term *tantra* (Tib. *rgyud*; pronounced "gyü") refers to systems of practice and meditation derived from esoteric texts emphasizing cognitive transformation through visualization, symbols, and ritual. These in turn gave rise to a vast commentarial literature, as well as oral traditions, and tantric practices, ideas, and images today permeate all aspects of Tibetan Buddhism. The root texts of this system are generally called "tantras"; most of these highlight a particular buddha who is the focus of ritual and meditative practices (in the *Hevajra Tantra*, for example, the buddha Hevajra is the central figure).

Although many of the fundamental treatises of this tradition are called tantras, there are some that do not contain the term "tantra" in the title, and there are some nontantric works that do. Each order of Tibetan Buddhism has its distinctive tantric practices, and individual lineages are often based on particular tantras or on groups of tantras that are considered to be related.

Tantric Buddhism is often referred to by its adherents as the Vajra Vehicle (*rDo rje'i theg pa, Vajrayāna*). The *vajra* (Tib. *rdo rje*; pronounced "dorjé") is an important symbol in the tantras: it is described as the hardest substance, something that is pure and unbreakable, like the omniscient wisdom of a buddha. Iconographically, the vajra is a five-pointed scepter that represents the method aspect of a buddha's realization. In tantric images, it is commonly held in the right hand by a buddha or bodhisattva, and a bell is held in the left hand. The bell denotes the wisdom aspect, and the two arms are often crossed, symbolizing the inseparable union of method and wisdom in the mind of a buddha. According to the *Vajra Crown Tantra* (*Vajraśekhara-tantra*), a vajra is "adamantine, hard, non-empty, with a nature that is imperturbable and indivisible; because it cannot be burned and is indestructible and empty, it is called 'vajra.'"[22]

Tantric Buddhism is also referred to as (1) the Method Vehicle because it contains numerous special techniques for rapid attainment of buddhahood and (2) the Effect Vehicle because it takes the final result of Buddhist practice—buddhahood—as the path and trains directly in the attributes of awakening. Vajrayāna is considered by its adherents to be a separate vehicle, along with Hīnayāna and Mahāyāna, and they believe it to be the supreme Buddhist system. It follows the general outlines of Indian Mahāyāna (which tantric exegetes often refer to as (1) the Sūtra Vehicle because it is based on the Mahāyāna sūtras or (2) Perfection Vehicle because it enjoins the gradual cultivation of the perfections as the path to buddhahood) and also valorizes the bodhisattva as its ideal, but Vajrayāna claims to have special and more effective methods of practice that can greatly shorten the path to buddhahood. As in the standard Mahāyāna, tantric bodhisattvas cultivate the six perfections, follow the five paths and ten levels, and their training also culminates in the awakening of a buddha, but highest yoga tantra texts maintain that practitioners can complete the path in one human lifetime instead of the three countless eons required for bodhisattvas of the Perfection Vehicle.[23]

Origins of Vajrayāna

Most tantras claim to have been spoken by Śākyamuni Buddha, or sometimes by other buddhas. This assertion is accepted by most Tibetan Buddhists but is generally rejected by contemporary historically oriented scholars, because no reliable evidence supports the appearance of tantras for at least a mil-

22 *Vajraśekhara-tantra*, To. 480.149a7–b1. Quoted in David Snellgrove, "The Notion of Divine Kingship in Tantric Buddhism," *La Regalitá Sacra—Contributi al Tema dell' VIII Congresso Internazionale di Storia delle Religioni* (Leiden: E. J. Brill, 1959), vol. 2, 104–105. In some contexts, the vajra is also a thunderbolt that is used to defeat enemies, or a diamond, and in texts of the highest yoga tantra class, the vajra is often equated with the penis.

23 Highest yoga tantra is one of the four standard divisions of tantric texts, which are discussed below.

lennium after the death of Śākyamuni. The discrepancy between the time of the Buddha and the period of Vajrayāna's flourishing in India has also been noted by Tibetan historians, and Tāranātha (1575–1635) attempts to explain it away by stating that Śākyamuni taught the tantras during his lifetime, but some were passed on in secret from master to disciple, while others were hidden in the Heaven of the Thirty-Three or Tuṣita until humans were ready to receive them.[24] The origins of tantra are extremely obscure, and there are numerous theories concerning when, where, and by whom various texts were composed.

There are no records from the Buddha's time that suggest he gave teachings resembling developed Vajrayāna. The tantras only began to appear in India toward the end of the seventh century—over a millennium after the Buddha's passing—and new ones continued to be composed until the twelfth century, and possibly later. It is clear from Tibetan records that when Buddhism was first disseminated in Tibet during the ninth and tenth centuries tantric texts and practices were well established in India and that many of the monastic universities that were centers for the transmission of the dharma were also centers of Vajrayāna study and practice.

Vajrayāna incorporated elements of earlier Buddhist traditions, including doctrines and practices. For example, tantric texts presuppose the doctrine of emptiness, which is central to the Madhyamaka and Yogācāra schools of Indian Buddhism, and places a high value on skill in means (the ability to adapt the dharma to different audiences), which is a core theme in a number of Mahāyāna sūtras. The symbol of the vajra predates Buddhism, as does the use of mantras, symbolic diagrams, and fire rituals (*sbyin sreg, homa*), all of which are central to Vajrayāna. Before the late seventh or early eighth centuries, however, there is no evidence of anything resembling the elaborate systems of doctrine and practice that characterized the developed Vajrayāna, nor are there records of adherents proclaiming it as a separate vehicle.

Whatever their origins, it is clear that the production of the new tantric texts in India—and the claim that these had been taught during the time of Śākyamuni—generated both great interest and strong opposition. These

24 A. Schiefner, ed., *Tāranātha's History of Buddhism* (Simla, 1970), p. 82. These realms feature prominently in Buddhist cosmology. They are transcendent spheres in which advanced bodhisattvas reside.

reactions are also found in the writings of contemporary Western scholars. Some view tantra as a development that accords with the ideals and doctrines of Mahāyāna, while others consider it to be a new phenomenon that marks a major paradigm shift. Some early Western researchers—apparently shocked by the presence of sexual imagery and practices, as well as a plethora of demonic figures—characterized tantra as the final degeneration of Indian Buddhism, a corruption of the ideals and practices of the dharma of Śākyamuni.

These thoughts are not, however, shared by Tibetan scholars, who generally view tantra as the supreme of all Buddhist teachings and who consider tantric practices to be the shortest and most effective path to buddhahood. Tantric texts and practices are considered by Tibetans to be a part of Mahāyāna, since they emphasize both the path of the bodhisattva, which leads to the supreme goal of buddhahood, and the central importance of compassion, which is the primary motivating factor in the bodhisattva's pursuit of awakening. As David Snellgrove has noted, however, tantric texts were not accepted wholesale in Tibet, and in order for a work to be acknowledged as authoritative Tibetan scholars generally required validation in the form of a Sanskrit original.[25]

Moreover, there was some opposition to the tantras during the early part of the first dissemination of Buddhism in Tibet, and two kings, Tri Songdétsen and Relbachen, forbade their translation into Tibetan. Later, in the eleventh century, the *Official Edict* catalogue of Yéshé Ö characterized such tantric practices as sexual union (*sbyor ba*) and "deliverance" (*sgrol ba*, which involved "liberating" beings from cyclic existence by killing them) as heretical and rejected tantras that contained descriptions of them. The famed translator Rinchen Sangpo (958-1055) made similar claims in his *Refutation of Errors regarding Secret Mantra*.[26] Such controversies continue today, and

25 David Snellgrove, *Indo-Tibetan Buddhism* (Boston: Shambhala, 1987), vol. 1, 118.

26 For more information on controversies regarding authentic tantric practices, see David Seyfort Ruegg, "Problems in the Transmission of Vajrayāna Buddhism in the Western Himalaya about the Year 1000," *Acta Indologica* 6 (1984), pp. 369–381. Samten Karmay discusses and translates Yéshé Ö's *Official Edict* in "The Ordinance of Lha Bla-ma Ye-shes-'od," Michael Aris and Aung San Suu Kyi, eds., *Tibetan Studies in Honour of Hugh Richardson* (Warminster: Aris & Philips, 1980), pp. 150–162.

Tibetan exegetes tend to construe the more outrageous passages in tantric texts symbolically.

The tantras commonly employ the opening formula of sūtras, "Thus have I heard at one time . . ." and are sometimes situated in Indian locations found in the Hīnayāna and Mahāyāna discourses, but in others the Buddha is said to reside in transcendental realms, and often engages in activities that he proscribed in his discourses and the vinaya. The *Hevajra Tantra* (II.3,29), for example, begins by asserting that the Buddha "dwelt in the vagina of the Vajrayoginī who is the body, speech, and mind of all buddhas." He tells the assembled bodhisattvas, "You should kill living beings, speak lying words, take things that are not given, and have sex with many women." They are so scandalized to see the Buddha *in flagrante delicto* and uttering such apparently scandalous words that they collectively faint. He magically revives them and informs them that the new teachings are more advanced versions of what they had previously learned. He then explains that these teachings are to be understood symbolically: "killing living beings" involves cultivating "singleness of thought"; "speaking lying words" refers to the vow to save all sentient beings; "what is not given" is a woman's bliss (presumably in sexual yoga); and "frequenting others' wives" is meditation focused on Nairātmyā, Hevajra's consort.

The Buddha explains that in the final analysis there is no difference between cyclic existence and nirvana (*'khor 'das dbyer med, saṃsāra-nirvāṇa-abheda*) and that the goal of tantric practice is to become indifferent to all notions of good and bad, pure and impure, permitted and proscribed: "There is nothing that one may not do, and nothing that one may not eat. There is nothing that one may not think or say, nothing that is either pleasant or unpleasant" (I.7, 24).

Tantra as a Branch of Mahāyāna

Sūtra and Tantra

Tantras differ from other Mahāyāna texts primarily in the area of method: they contain practices, symbols, and teachings that are not found in other Mahāyāna works, and these are held by their adherents to be more potent and effective than those of the Perfection Vehicle. Through tantric practice, one is able to overcome afflictions and deluded thoughts, progress rapidly through the Buddhist paths, and attain the state of buddhahood in order to benefit others.

Vajrayāna focuses on ritual, visualization, and symbols in order to effect rapid transformation to the state of buddhahood. Many tantrists even claim that it is *only* possible to become a buddha through practice of highest yoga tantra. The Dalai Lama, for instance, asserts that "one must finally engage in Mantra [another name for tantric practice] in order to become a Buddha."[27] As we saw in earlier sections, this claim runs counter to the popular biographies of Śākyamuni, which make no mention of tantra. This discrepancy is explained away by stating that although Śākyamuni *appeared* to take rebirth in India and attain awakening, in reality he had become awakened in the distant past. His birth, life in the palace, pursuit of awakening, etc. were really only a display put on for the benefit of people of limited intellect. Like all buddhas, he attained buddhahood through the special practices of highest yoga tantra.

In the *Compendium of the Truth of All Tathāgatas*, it is related that as Siddhārtha Gautama sat under the Tree of Awakening he was roused from his meditation by the buddhas of the ten directions, who informed him that it is impossible to attain buddhahood without engaging in the sexual yogas of highest yoga tantra. Realizing that this was the case, he left his physical body under the tree and traveled to a transcendent tantric realm, where he received consecrations and engaged in sexual yogas with a consort named Tilottamā. He then returned to Bodh Gaya and resumed his display.[28]

Motivation

Although in Tibet tantra is generally considered to be the culmination of Buddhist teachings, it is not suitable for everyone. Tantric practice is a pow-

27 Tenzin Gyatso, H.H. the Fourteenth Dalai Lama, in *Tantra in Tibet*, tr. Jeffrey Hopkins (London: George Allen & Unwin, 1977), p. 69.

28 The passage is translated in Snellgrove, *Indo-Tibetan Buddhism*, vol. 1, 120. In another version, he practiced highest yoga tantra with Tilottamā during the life before the one in which he manifested as a buddha. As a result of this practice, he was already fully awakened before taking birth in India, and his whole life was a manifestation for the benefit of others. See also Mkhas-grub-rje's *Fundamentals of the Buddhist Tantras*, Lessing and Wayman, eds. (The Hague/Paris, 1968), pp. 28–37.

erful and effective means of bringing about spiritual transformation, but for this very reason it is also dangerous. Thus Tibetan teachers contend that it is only appropriate for certain exceptional individuals, while others should follow the slower but less dangerous path of the Mahāyāna sūtra system or of Hīnayāna.

What sort of people are suitable receptacles for tantric teachings? According to the Dalai Lama, only those with unusually strong compassion and an overpowering urge to attain buddhahood in order to benefit others should undertake the training of Vajrayāna:

> A person who has practised the stages of sūtra and wishes to attain quickly the state of a blessed Buddha *should* enter into the Secret Mantra Vehicle that can easily bestow realisation of Buddhahood. However, you cannot seek Buddhahood for yourself, engaging in Mantra in order to become unusual.... You must develop great compassion from the very orb of your heart for all sentient beings traveling in cyclic existence.... You need to have a very strong mind wishing to free all sentient beings from suffering and its causes.[29]

Practitioners of tantra must have greater compassion—and greater intelligence—than those who follow the sūtra path. The special methods and powerful techniques of Vajrayāna are intended for those whose compassion is so acute that they cannot bear to wait for a long time in order to benefit others.

The Faults of Cyclic Existence

In addition to the motivation of compassion, tantric practitioners must be perceptive enough to recognize the faults of cyclic existence. Ordinary, ignorant beings are caught up in fleeting and transitory pleasures and fail to recognize the pervasiveness of suffering and the inevitability of death. Intelligent people who meditate on the nature of things, however, recognize the unsatisfactoriness of cyclic existence and generate a strong desire to escape it.

29 *Tantra in Tibet*, p. 18.

In common with the exoteric sūtra path, tantric texts teach that transmigratory existence is a vicious cycle that is driven by afflicted desires and mistaken thoughts. The minds of ordinary beings run after fleeting stimuli and are easily distracted by things that appear to promise satisfaction but which in the end turn out to be disappointing.

While most exoteric Buddhist texts advise practitioners to reduce desire in order to attain liberation, tantric treatises propose to incorporate the energy of desire into the path. The problem lies not in desire *per se*, but rather in a misdirection of the energy of desire toward objects that lead to suffering and bondage.

Tantric Buddhism accepts the idea found in many Buddhist texts that buddhas have overcome desire, but holds that the path to extinction of desire does not necessitate its suppression. In fact, since desire is a very powerful force in human beings, suppressing it requires the expenditure of a great deal of energy and diligent practice over an extended period of time. The skillful means of Vajrayāna, however, provide methods to redirect this energy by utilizing it in the spiritual path, so that desire itself becomes a means to overcome desire. This process is compared to the way that two sticks can be rubbed together to create a fire that consumes them.

This does not mean, however, that tantra involves unrestrained wallowing in pleasure. Rather, desire and bliss are carefully channeled through meditative practices, and they are used in very specific ways. The path of tantra involves great discipline and requires keen intelligence, and it is based on a strong wish to help others. It has nothing to do with sensual indulgence.

Desire and Skillful Means

Human beings want happiness and seek to avoid suffering. These are accepted as legitimate goals by Vajrayāna, but the methods commonly used to achieve them are rejected. Most people seek pleasure for themselves alone and look for it in material objects, the approval of others, interpersonal relationships, etc. None of these things are able to provide lasting contentment, since they are impermanent and thus subject to change and death.

The problem lies in looking for fulfillment in external things, since true happiness is found in the mind. Tantric texts claim that the human mind contains the seeds of both suffering and of lasting joy, and that one's state of mind determines which one one will experience. Unlike ascetic traditions that seek to find satisfaction through difficult or painful meditative practices, Vajrayāna cultivates blissful mental states. In tantra, one actualizes progressively deeper understanding of the nature of reality through experiencing pleasurable cognitions, gaining control over physical and mental energies, and conjoining blissful consciousnesses with realization of the nature of reality.

Through the skillful methods of Vajrayāna, meditators are able to cultivate enjoyment in a way that aids in spiritual progress. Afflicted grasping and desires based on mistaken ideas are the problem, not happiness and pleasure. If the pursuit of contentment can be separated from afflictive emotions, then it can be incorporated into the path and will even become a powerful aid to the attainment of awakening. The *Hevajra Tantra*, for example, states,

> That by which the world is bound,
> By the same things it is released from bondage.
> But the world is deluded and does not understand this truth,
> And one who does not possess this truth cannot attain perfection.[30]

Tantra, however, is not concerned merely with cultivation of pleasure, nor is its purview restricted to actions and practices that are traditionally associated with "religion." Tantra proposes to incorporate all actions, all thoughts, all emotions into the path. Nothing in itself is pure or impure, good or bad, mundane or transcendent; things only appear to us in these ways because of preconceived ideas. In the Vajrayāna systems, any action—even walking, eating, defecating, or sleeping—can be an element of the spiritual path. Tantric practitioners seek to overcome the pervasive sense of ordinariness that colors our perceptions of daily life.

30 David Snellgrove, ed., *The Hevajra-tantra* (London: Oxford University Press, 1959), I.9, 19: vol. 2, 34–35.

Tantric Symbols

Maṇḍalas

The Sanskrit term *maṇḍala* (*dkyil 'khor*) literally means "circle," both in the sense of a circular diagram and a surrounding retinue. In Buddhist usage the term encompasses both senses, because it refers to circular diagrams that often incorporate depictions of deities and their surroundings. The maṇḍala represents a sacred realm—often the celestial palace of a buddha—and it contains symbols and images that illustrate aspects of the awakened psycho-physical personality of the buddha and that indicate Buddhist themes and concepts. The maṇḍala serves as a representation of an awakened mind that is free of all obstacles, and in the context of tantric practice it is a symbol of the state that meditators are trying to attain.

Maṇḍalas often consist of a series of concentric circles, enclosed by a square, which in turn has a circular boundary. The square contains a gateway in the middle of each side, the main one facing east, with three other openings at each of the other cardinal directions. They represent entrances to the central palace of the main deity and are based on the design of the classical Indian four-sided temple. Such maṇḍalas are elaborate floor plans of the palace, viewed from the top. The portals, however, are often laid down flat, as are outer walls. These portals are lavishly decorated with tantric symbols. The architecture of the maṇḍala represents both the nature of reality and the order of an awakened mind. The two-dimensional blueprint is then used as a template for visualization. The image, emanated from the empty nature of mind through the power of creative visualization, is intended to evoke attitudes and understandings that correspond to its internal symbolic structure.

The middle of the maṇḍala represents the inner sanctum of the main deity and is the sacred center of the whole image. There are innumerable variations on the primary theme, some of which are very simple, with a single deity dominating the center, while others are complex and may contain hundreds of attendants, buddhas, mythical creatures, symbols, and landscapes. All are intended to represent the state of awakening iconographically, and the palace is a creation of the awakened mind of the main buddha.

Practitioners are regularly reminded, however, that the figures in the maṇḍala have no real ontological status; they are representations of the mental qualities toward which tantric adepts aspire and are intended to provide templates for mental transformation, but they are empty of inherent existence. This is also true of demons and wrathful deities, which represent factors of human consciousness that are transmuted through meditation into virtuous qualities.

In tantric literature, there are descriptions of various types of maṇḍalas, some of which exist in concrete form as painted canvas maṇḍalas or sand maṇḍalas that are used as aids in meditation or as the focal points of initiation ceremonies. In some texts, the external maṇḍalas are said to be representations of natural maṇḍalas, which are nonphysical and represent the awakened qualities of buddhahood. Other maṇḍalas are internal: meditational maṇḍalas are visualized by the mind of a practitioner as three-dimensional figures. In tantric theory, the body itself is also considered to be a maṇḍala and is the crucible of training designed to transform it into the body of a buddha.

Once constructed and consecrated, maṇḍalas are believed to be imbued with the presence of the relevant buddha(s) and thus become focal points for devotion and visualized offerings. They are also thought to have magical power and can prolong life, bring wealth, protect against evil, and are often worn as amulets.

Mantras

Mantras are invocations to buddhas, magical spells, prayers, or a combination of these. Tantric practitioners repeat them in order to forge karmic connections between themselves and meditational deities and to effect cognitive restructuring through internalizing the divine attributes that the mantra represents.

The use of mantras is central to Vajrayāna practice, and so the system is often referred to by its adherents as the "Mantra Vehicle" or "Secret Mantra Vehicle." Mantra repetition is not simply an external activity in which one vocalizes sounds; it is primarily an act intended to awaken the cognitive potential of the meditator.

The external vocalization of the sounds of the mantra serves as a focus for mental development. By concentrating on the significance of the mantra as explained by their gurus and opening themselves to their transforming power, meditators awaken their own latent potential for awakening. Through this the sounds of their bodies come to be perceived as divine sounds, and their speech becomes the speech of a buddha.

In some Hindu systems, mantras are said to be primordial sounds that possess power in and of themselves. In Tibetan Buddhist tantra, mantras have no such inherent power—unless they are recited by a person with a focused mind, they are only sounds. For people with the proper attitude, however, they can be powerful tools that aid in the process of transformation.

Entering Tantric Practice

Initiation

Vajrayāna is presented as a secret system by its texts and practitioners, and so it is not surprising that special initiations (*dbang, abhiṣeka*) are required in order to enter the tantra path. The bestowal of initiation is a necessary precondition for tantric practice, since this forges a special bond between the student, the lama, and the meditational deity (*yi dam, iṣṭa-devatā*). Nor is initiation open to everyone: only those who are judged by the teacher to possess the necessary intelligence and spiritual aptitude are considered fit for initiation. For people who lack the necessary qualifications, tantra is dangerous, and the texts repeatedly warn that such people can greatly harm themselves if they enter into Vajrayāna practice.

Although tantra is said by its adherents to be an effective and rapid means of gaining awakening, it should not be taught to everyone, only to those who demonstrate the necessary prerequisites. This is hardly a surprising attitude, and analogies may be found in other areas. For example, jet airplanes are effective means of getting from one place to another very quickly, but it is extremely dangerous to pilot them without the necessary initiation of extensive flight training under a qualified instructor. In addition, admission to such training is generally restricted to people with the preconditions for successful piloting, such as good eyesight, coordination, mental stability, and so forth. Operation of jet airplanes by people without proper training or who are physically or mentally impaired could be disastrous, and so potential pilots are screened thoroughly and regularly tested to ensure that their skills have not deteriorated.

Tantric initiation is intended to accomplish many of the same goals. Lamas should test those who desire initiation, making sure that their commitment is genuine and is motivated by an altruistic determination to attain buddhahood and not by desire to impress others through acquiring magical powers or by other negative goals. If one wrongly enters the tantric path, one can bring great harm to oneself and others, and so lamas are warned to screen candidates carefully.

Aspirants who are judged to be suitable receptacles for tantric initiations are sworn to secrecy. Initiates are required to take a series of vows (*dam tshig, samaya*), one of which is not to reveal tantric teachings openly. The promised retributions for breaking the vows include painful suffering in "vajra hells" reserved for those who transgress their tantric promises.

Despite the solemnity of the vows and the fearsomeness of the threatened punishments for transgression, initiation is generally viewed with joyful anticipation, because the aspirant is being established on the fastest and most effective path to awakening. Initiation empowers the initiate and awakens the hidden potential for buddhahood that lies dormant in everyone.

All beings possess the "buddha nature," meaning that they have the capacity to perfect themselves and become buddhas. It is the source of all intelligence and good qualities, and is the ground of every being's personality. The basic nature of mind, as we have seen, is clear light, pure luminosity untainted by any mental constructions. During initiation, the lama introduces students to the nature of their own minds. The ideal student-teacher relationship is not, however, that of a master and a slave, but a true meeting of two minds. The teacher is a person who has successfully cultivated the esoteric teachings of tantra and thus actualized the latent potential of the buddha nature, and students possess the same potential and rely on the lama's instructions in order to attain the same level of realization themselves.

Initiation introduces students to a new vision of reality, one that is not bound by ordinary conceptuality. Nothing is conceived as substantially existent or permanent, and everything is known to be the interplay of luminosity and emptiness. This reality is open and expansive; there are no limits, and so it is also frightening at first. It is as though the firm ground under one's feet has been removed, and one is set adrift in a realm of infinite possibilities, with no rules, no boundaries, and no certainties.

Tantric initiation is often a complex ritual involving detailed visualizations, prayers and supplications, offerings, and special ritual implements and substances. The purpose is to establish the initiate in the proper frame of mind, forge a karmic bond with the lama and meditational deity, purify defilements, grant permission to practice a particular tantra, and to give instruction concerning how this should be done.

For serious practitioners of Vajrayāna, initiation is not something that is received only once. Tantric texts speak of the great power of the process, and initiates are urged to participate in initiation again and again, since each experience of these rites has the potential to confer profound blessings on trainees and inspire them to pursue their practice with renewed vigor.

Deity Yoga as a Union of Method and Wisdom

Deity yoga is said by its adherents to be superior to sūtra practice because it utilizes a "union of method and wisdom." Wisdom refers to a consciousness that realizes emptiness, the lack of inherent existence of all phenomena. Method refers to one's motivation and the activities that one performs for the benefit of others in order to establish them in awakening. Both are essential aspects of the awakened mind of a buddha. According to tantric texts, practitioners of sūtra train in these two characteristics separately, which means that each is cultivated independently. Because of this, the sūtra path requires a very long time to complete. Tantra, however, has methods in which one develops both at the same time, and so they quickly become manifested in the continuum of one's consciousness. This is accomplished by the practice of deity yoga, in which the subtle consciousness that meditates on emptiness is actualized in a physical form embodying compassion.

As an analogy, if one wishes to learn to play the flute, it might be helpful to study flute music, listen to great performances, read the biographies of accomplished musicians, study the dynamics of how the flute produces sounds, and so forth; but if one only does these things, one may know a great deal about the flute but will never master the technique of actually playing it. It would be far more beneficial to actually begin playing the flute under the guidance of a qualified teacher. Through engaging in training, and through diligent practice, one may eventually become skilled in flute playing. From the point of view of tantra, sūtra practitioners are like people wishing to play the flute who only train in related activities. They have greater understanding than those who never begin instruction at all, but their progress is very slow because they fail to familiarize themselves with the effect they are trying to achieve. In the context of tantric practice, this goal is buddhahood, and although engagement in such concordant qualities as the six perfections, skill in means, etc. is very beneficial, it will not bring about the state of a fully awakened buddha without the special techniques of tantra, in which one actually cultivates the bodies of a buddha.

The perfections and other bodhisattva practices are effective means of spiritual development, but they bear no resemblance to the form body of a buddha, and thus they cannot become a form body. A form body is a manifestation of the wisdom consciousness of a buddha in a form embodying compassion, and this can only be developed by an awakened consciousness in which direct perception of emptiness and the mind of awakening are conjoined. Proponents of Vajrayāna assert that this is only accomplished by means of the practice of deity yoga. In deity yoga, the consciousness perceiving emptiness is manifested as a buddha. The buddha's wisdom consciousness, motivated by compassion, is a projection of one's own mind and serves as a template for one's development. The appearance of the deity develops into a buddha's form body, while one's mind develops into a truth body, and thus both bodies are complete in one consciousness.

Sādhanas

Central to this system is the use of meditational rituals called "means of achievement" (*sgrub thabs, sādhana*), in which one combines prayers, visualizations, hand gestures, and bodily movements that represent the awakened aspects of the mind of a particular buddha. These practices are based on meditational manuals that outline ritual practices for particular deities. Sādhanas describe the qualities of the deity and its retinue, contain recitations of mantras and prayers, and they are connected with visualization of the deity's maṇḍala. By repeatedly performing the prescribed activities of the means of achievement, meditators enhance their powers of visualization, until eventually the entire diagram appears clearly in their minds.

During the process of emanating a maṇḍala, the meditator praises the deity, asks for blessings, and envisions the deity's maṇḍala, but is not simply a devout supplicant. The meditation process requires that meditators view themselves as inseparable from the deity and as possessing all the attributes of a fully awakened buddha. Thus, they are not simply praising someone else's good qualities but are using the meditation to develop the same attributes themselves. Through repeated familiarization with the rituals of the means of achievement, meditators begin to approximate the state of awakening.

Means of achievement range from simple rites that can be done in a relatively short time to elaborate combinations of prayers, offerings, and visualizations of vast numbers of deities in various patterns. They generally begin with recitation of the refuge prayer and an indication of one's intention to manifest the mind of awakening. This is followed by visualization of the central deity, generally accompanied by other buddhas and various attendants.

The next phase involves paying homage to the deity and repetition of his/her mantra, and one may imagine that all sentient beings are also participating in the practice and deriving merit from it. The deity is viewed as responding positively to one's prayers and bestowing blessings. In the next phase one visualizes the deity being dissolved into emptiness, and one abides in nonconceptual contemplation of suchness. The concluding part of the ritual involves dedication of the merit generated by it to all sentient beings and hoping that they benefit from one's practice.

This practice enables meditators to reconstruct the world in accordance with the meditation. Those who become adepts know that they are no longer bound by the fetters of ordinariness; their surroundings become the environment of a buddha. Their companions are viewed as a buddha's retinue, and their actions are the compassionate activities of a buddha.

Advanced meditators develop the ability to create environments of their own choosing, and they are able to transcend the sufferings that seem so real to ordinary beings who are bound by mundane conceptions. According to Tsong Khapa, for one who attains advanced levels of meditation painful cognitions no longer occur, no matter what external experiences one encounters. All of one's cognitions are a union of bliss and emptiness. One recognizes that nothing is inherently what it appears to be. Whatever occurs is perceived by one's unshakably blissful consciousness as the sport of luminosity and emptiness, and so

> for a Bodhisattva who has attained the meditative stabilisation of bliss pervading all phenomena, only a feeling of pleasure arises with respect to all objects; pain and neutrality do not occur, even though [pieces from his body] the size of a small coin (*kārṣhāpaṇa*) are cut or even though his body is crushed by elephants, only a discrimination of bliss is maintained.[31]

Tantric texts stress that such bodhisattvas are not creating a delusional system in order to hide from the harsher aspects of reality. Rather, they are transforming reality, making it conform to an ideal archetype. Since all phenomena are empty of inherent existence, they have no fixed nature. No one ever apprehends an object as it is in its true nature, because there is no such nature. Even if phenomena had fixed essences, we would still never be able to perceive them, since all we ever experience are our cognitions of objects, which are overlaid with conceptions about them. All our perceptions are *ideas about* things, and not real things. These ideas are also empty, arising from nothingness and immediately dissolving again into nothingness, leaving nothing behind. Tantric adepts develop the ability to reconstitute "reality," which is completely malleable for those who train in yogas involving blissful consciousnesses realizing emptiness. The sense of bliss pervades all their cognitions, and their understanding of emptiness allows them to generate minds that are manifestations of bliss and emptiness.

The Four Classes of Tantra

Tibetan exegetes have developed numerous classification systems for tantric texts, the most common of which is a fourfold division into: (1) action tantras; (2) performance tantras; (3) yoga tantras; and (4) highest yoga tantras. This method of differentiating tantras was developed in the thirteenth and fourteenth centuries and used to classify these texts in the definitive version of the Tibetan Buddhist canon by the scholar Pudön. The system is based on the types of practices emphasized in a particular tantra and the relative importance of external rituals or internal yogas.

31 *Tantra in Tibet*, p. 143.

Action tantras are primarily taught for meditators who require external activities. The special trainees of action tantras are people who lack the capacity for profound meditation on emptiness but are able to engage enthusiastically in external rituals and activities.

Action tantra trainees engage in activities in which symbolic representations of aspects of the path are created or acted out. For example, one may make or buy a painting of a deity, place it in a special spot and make offerings to it, imagining that the deity is actually present there. Other activities include ritual bathing in which one envisions the external activity of washing as purifying mental afflictions. The activities of action tantra are designed for those who are not adept at internal visualization and who can benefit from having physical symbols as focal points for their meditation.

Practitioners of action tantra understand that in reality all phenomena are an undifferentiable union of appearance and emptiness, but on the conventional level of practice they perceive themselves and the meditational deity as separate entities. They view the deity as a master or lord and themselves as servants, performing acts of devotion in stylized ritual dramas involving activities of body and speech.

Performance tantras equally emphasize external activities and internal yoga. The main practices of performance tantra involve mentally creating an image of oneself as an awakened being and also generating the form of a deity in front of oneself as a template. One views oneself and the deity as companions or friends, and one strives to emulate it. One also chants the mantra of the deity and endeavors to perfect one's ability to visualize it without mental fluctuation. There are two aspects to this meditation: a yoga with signs and a signless yoga. The first type involves stabilizing the mind by developing one-pointed concentration on the deity, the letters of its mantra (visualized at the heart), its hand-gestures (*phyag rgya, mudrā*), and its form. Signless yoga focuses on the deity's final nature—emptiness—and not on external characteristics.

In *yoga tantra* one visualizes oneself as an actual buddha, and not merely as a devotee or companion of a buddha. Yoga tantras emphasize internal yoga. One visualizes oneself and the archetypal deity as separate beings, and then one causes the deity to enter oneself.

In *highest yoga tantra* one develops a profound awareness of one's body as being composed of subtle energies called winds (*rlung, prāṇa*) and drops (*thig le, bindu*) which move through a network of seventy-two thousand channels (*rtsa, nāḍī*). One then generates oneself as a fully awakened buddha composed entirely of these subtle energies and possessing a buddha's wisdom consciousness.

Practitioners of yoga tantra view all phenomena as being naturally free from the signs of mental projection and as manifestations of luminosity and emptiness. On the conventional level, meditators train in perceiving all appearances as maṇḍalas of deities. Although trainees of yoga tantra engage in some external activities, ritual is viewed as being symbolic of the primary practice of internal yoga. In yoga tantra one first generates a vivid appearance of the deity, together with its retinue, contemplating both its wondrous form and exalted attributes, and then one absorbs the deity into oneself, imagining that one becomes merged with it.

Highest yoga tantra is divided into two stages: the stage of generation and the stage of completion. Both are factors in the transformation of one's mind and body into the mind and body of a buddha. In the stage of generation, one creates a vivid image of a deity, and in the stage of completion one transforms oneself into an actual deity possessing the exalted form and awakened mind of a buddha.

There are three primary prerequisites for entering the stage of generation: (1) previous practice of paths common to both sūtra and tantra; (2) initiation into a highest yoga tantra; and (3) taking on tantric pledges and vows. The first prerequisite entails correct motivation: the mind of awakening. The practice of the common paths serves to establish the proper orientation and attitudes. This is important, because in order to endure the rigors of highest yoga tantra one should have a clear idea of why one is traveling the path to awakening and what one's goals are. With this as a basis, one trains in the six perfections and in the activities of bodhisattvas.

Proponents of tantra claim that all the practices of sūtra are included in tantra, although tantra transcends sūtra because of its profundity and effectiveness. Thus, in tantra one cultivates the qualities characteristic of bodhisattvas—generosity, ethics, patience, effort, concentration, wisdom, etc.—but one develops them much more quickly through engaging in deity yoga. The techniques of tantra supplement the bodhisattva's training, but they do not contradict or supersede the wish to attain awakening for the benefit of others. Rather, they are practical enhancements that allow meditators to progress more quickly by giving them access to subtle levels of consciousness in order to bring about profound transformations.

To enter into the training program of the stage of generation, one must first receive the vase initiation. Practice of the stage of completion requires the vase initiation, plus the secret initiation, the knowledge initiation, and the word initiation.

These two stages are intimately connected in that the generation stage is a necessary precondition for the completion stage. The generation stage prepares the mind for the completion stage by gradually enhancing the clarity of one's visualizations until they are made manifest in the completion stage.

The conferral of initiation serves as an empowerment, which creates a karmic connection between the student, the deities of the maṇḍalas, and the lama. There are also special tantric pledges that initiates are required to take. These hold students to a strict code of conduct and provide an ethical basis that is essential to successful tantric practice. This is important, because many of the techniques of highest yoga tantra are dangerous, and the vows serve as a counterbalance to tendencies toward possible negative attitudes and behaviors.

The Stage of Generation

In the stage of generation one trains the mind with imaginative visualizations. One creates a vivid image of a deity that possesses all the physical marks of a buddha, as well as its mental qualities. The purpose of this stage is to develop one's imaginative powers to such a degree that one's mental creations become real. In the stage of completion, one finalizes the process by transforming oneself in accordance with the visualizations of the stage of generation.

This system conceives trainees in terms of a mystical physiology. The body contains seventy-two thousand energy channels, through which winds circulate. The most important ones are a central channel, which is roughly contiguous with the spine, and a left and right channel that wrap around the central channel at certain points and constrict the movements of winds in the channels. These constriction points are called *cakras* (*rtsa 'khor*).

In tantric physiology, consciousnesses are said to travel throughout the body "mounted" on the winds, which serve as their support. Consciousnesses cannot function without the support of the winds, but the winds lack direction without consciousnesses. Because of this, consciousnesses by themselves are said to be like people without legs, while winds by themselves are like blind people. Each needs the other, and they function in tandem, with winds providing movement and consciousnesses providing direction. Because of this intimate connection, whatever affects one also affects the other, and so meditators wishing to gain control over consciousness must also learn to influence the movements of winds.

In tantric meditation, one learns to manipulate the winds in order to bring about particular types of consciousness. In the system of highest yoga tantra, one acquires the ability to control them with great precision in order to gain access to very subtle levels of mind. In the stage of generation, yogins cause the winds to move into the central channel, remain there, and then dissolve. The dissolution of the winds results in profound bliss and the manifestation of subtle consciousnesses, which can be used to bring about specific realizations, such as direct cognition of emptiness.

Through learning to influence the movements of winds, meditators simulate the process of death, in which progressively subtler levels of mind manifest as the winds dissolve in stages. With the dissolution of winds, a succession of consciousnesses appears, each more subtle than the last, until the arising of the "mind of clear light," which is the most subtle and basic of all minds. In ordinary death, the stages of this process occur involuntarily, but through the special techniques of highest yoga tantra yogins can cause the subtle minds to manifest under their conscious control.

The Stage of Completion

In the stage of completion, the meditator is actually transformed into the buddha that was visualized in the stage of generation. In this practice, one learns to visualize oneself as a deity with intense clarity and vividness, one's environment is perceived as the environment of a fully actualized buddha, and one develops the nonafflicted pride of a deity. In the stage of completion, one acquires the ability to cause winds to enter the central channel and dissolve in the "indestructible drop" in the center of the heart. This drop was created at birth from the fluids of one's father and mother, and it remains in the heart until death. As one causes winds to enter into it and dissolve, one experiences a profound bliss, and concomitantly one actualizes progressively subtler levels of mind. When all the winds have been dissolved in the indestructible drop, the mind of clear light manifests, and this can be used to cognize emptiness directly.

At this point, one is no longer bound by the physical and cognitive restraints of ordinary beings, and one attains a subtle body composed of winds in the form of a deity possessing all the physical marks of a buddha.

Tantric Seals

At advanced levels of the stage of completion, yogins utilize special sexual techniques that involve a "seal," or partner. In these practices, one visualizes oneself and one's partner as specific deities, and one's sexual union is used as a way of generating very subtle minds. According to tantric theory, in orgasm coarser levels of mind drop away, but most people do not see the potential meditative benefits of the experience. In the practices using seals, the occurrence of orgasm is conjoined with yogas that draw the winds into the central channel. The result is an indescribable sensation of bliss and direct perception of emptiness. The partner is referred to as a "seal" because the practice seals the realization that all phenomena are a union of bliss and emptiness.

The bliss of union—which is combined with the wisdom consciousness realizing emptiness—approximates the mental state of buddhas, who perceive all appearances as manifestations of luminosity and emptiness and who are untroubled by the vicissitudes of phenomenal reality. Sexual yogas often involve retention of semen by male practitioners. In such contexts, the semen is referred to as "mind of awakening," and the movement of subtle energies through the central channel is equated with generation of the aspiration to become a buddha.

Tantric texts stress that practice with consorts is not a form of sexual indulgence, but rather a technique of controlled visualization that uses the special bliss of sexual union. It is restricted to very advanced practitioners, yogins who have gained control over the emanation of a subtle body and have awakened the mystical heat energy, or *dumo* (*gtum mo, caṇḍālī*). Those who have not progressed to this level are not qualified to practice with an actual consort; people without the necessary prerequisites who mimic tantric sexual practices thinking that they are practicing Vajrayāna are simply deluded and may do themselves great harm. Sexual union is only appropriate to the highest levels of the stage of completion, and so those who have not developed sufficient realization and control over subtle energies are unable to generate the blissful wisdom consciousness realizing emptiness that is the basis for this practice. They may succeed in fooling others—or even themselves—but they will be utterly unable to use sexual energy in accordance with the practices of highest yoga tantra.

The Preliminary Practices

According to Tibetan Buddhism, ordinary beings are born into life situations in which they are destined to suffer and die. This is the result of former contaminated actions and afflictions, which have been accumulated since beginningless time. Because of this process, physical and mental afflictions are deeply rooted in sentient beings, and so it is generally considered necessary to prepare oneself for tantric practice by engaging in the "preliminary practices," or *ngöndro* (*sngon 'gro, pūrvagama*), in order to begin to reverse one's negative conditioning. These practices combine physical movements with visualization in order to transform the mind from one that is fixated on mundane concerns and desires into one that is primarily oriented toward religious practice for the benefit of others. Some teachers consider these preparatory trainings to be so essential to successful tantric practice that they will not give tantric initiations to those who have not completed them, and even teachers who are willing to waive them generally stress their importance. The preliminary practices are: (1) taking refuge; (2) prostration; (3) Vajrasattva meditation; (4) maṇḍala offering; and (5) guru yoga.

Taking Refuge

Before entering into the practice of tantra, it is necessary to "take refuge," a practice that is common to all schools of Buddhism. The theory behind it is based on the idea that people who are unhappy with their present circumstances should consider the causes of the dissatisfaction and evaluate possible solutions. According to Buddhism, the root cause of all the sufferings of cyclic existence is ignorance, which causes us mistakenly to imagine that transitory things like money, sex, power, possessions, or relationships will bring enduring joy and fulfillment. If we consider this widespread assumption, however, we find that many people who have such things in abundance are profoundly unhappy, and so it is clear that they offer no guarantee of satisfaction. The problem with seeking contentment in such things, according to Buddhist thinkers, is that they are transitory, impermanent, and subject to change, and so they cannot be a source of lasting happiness.

Another potential source of happiness lies in religious practice, and there are many religions that offer a path to salvation for their followers. Some, like Christianity and Islam, promise a blissful existence in a heaven for those who follow certain rules and who worship particular divinities. Others, like Jainism, hold that asceticism and self-denial are the keys to enduring contentment; in this system, people who undergo prolonged physical austerities eventually transcend all suffering and experience bliss. Buddhism, however, rejects these two options and contends that the route to lasting happiness lies in meditation that eliminates suffering through destroying the bases of suffering—ignorance and the afflictive emotions it engenders.

Many Buddhist texts caution, however, that most people cannot accomplish this on their own, because the afflictive emotions are so deeply ingrained that they color all our thoughts and distort our perceptions. In order to transcend them successfully, it is necessary to find a qualified spiritual guide and follow a path that, according to our best evidence, is able to bring trainees to a state of happiness. Buddhists, not surprisingly, contend that when one examines the available paths, one will conclude that Buddhism holds out the strongest possibility of true salvation.

Taking refuge vows indicates a formal commitment to Buddhist practice. One declares that one has decided to rely on the "three jewels" of Buddhism—the Buddha, the dharma, and the sangha (the community of Buddhist monks and nuns).

When one takes refuge, one declares that one believes, on the basis of the available evidence, that the three jewels are reliable guides and that the Buddhist path offers the best chance for salvation. The actual ceremony of taking refuge is a simple affair: generally the initiate, in the presence of a lama, declares three times, "I take refuge in the Buddha; I take refuge in the

Dharma; I take refuge in the Sangha." Those who make this declaration with conviction are Buddhists. Because one's main teacher plays a central role in tantric practice, tantric initiates commonly take refuge first in the guru and then in the three jewels. Initiates of highest yoga tantra also often take refuge in wisdom beings called ḍākinīs, who play a central role in the practice and dissemination of tantras of the highest yoga tantra class.

Whatever Buddhist path one follows, taking refuge is viewed as a necessary precondition, since it focuses the mind on the goal of Buddhist awakening, clearly identifies the guides one will follow, and forges a connection with the sources of refuge. Before entering into advanced tantric practice, it is customary to recite the refuge prayer at least one hundred thousand times.

Prostration

Prostration (*phyag 'tshal*) is a crucial preparatory activity in which one prostrates oneself on the floor, generally in front of an image, altar, painting, or some other religious symbol. Because it involves physical activity, it is considered to be particularly effective in overcoming negative physical karma. It requires a complete physical abasement of the individual before symbols of deities—who are viewed as completely surpassing the meditator in good qualities—and so it is a counteragent to false pride. In bowing down, the meditator recognizes the superior wisdom and compassion of buddhas and bodhisattvas and requests their aid in attaining their exalted state.

Prostration begins in a standing position. The practitioner's hands are in the "gem-holding position," in which the base of the palm and the tips of the fingers are touching, with a space between the middle of the palms. The thumbs are tucked in. The folded hands are raised above the head, and with them the practitioner touches either three or four points on the body. In the first method, one touches the crown of the head, throat, and heart, and in the second, the crown, forehead, throat, and heart are touched. Touching the crown symbolizes one's wish to attain the body of a buddha; touching the throat symbolizes one's goal of attaining the speech of a buddha; touching the heart symbolizes the aim of actualizing the mind of a buddha.

Because prostration combines physical movements with verbal recitation and mental visualizations, it simultaneously purifies the "three doors" of body, speech, and mind and provides a powerful counteragent to afflictions. When used as a preparatory practice for tantra, it is customary to perform one hundred thousand prostrations, but Tibetans commonly do many more. There is no outer limit to the amount of merit one may acquire, and so practitioners are encouraged to do as many as possible, since prostration serves to undermine the power of afflictive emotions. It is important to note that prostrations—as well as the other preliminary practices—are not performed only prior to entry into tantric practice. Because they serve to diminish the force of afflictions, they are said to be effective at all levels of the path, and it is common for even advanced meditators to begin retreats with prostrations and other practices in order to purify their minds and set the proper tone for religious practice. It is also common for committed tantrists to make them a part of their daily practices.

Vajrasattva Meditation

Vajrasattva (*rDo rje sems dpa'*) is a buddha associated with mental purification. The preliminary practice of Vajrasattva meditation involves picturing this deity at the crown of one's head and mentally associating the image with all the physical, mental, and spiritual perfections characteristic of fully awakened buddhas. One thinks of Vajrasattva as being identical with one's own root lama, who manifests in a form of purity as a sign of blessing.

There are many variations in this practice, and individual lineages have their own distinctive teachings. The description that follows is a short version that contains the most common aspects of the visualization process. At the beginning of a session of Vajrasattva meditation, one should find a quiet place free from distractions, assume a position in which the spine is straight, the eyes slightly open, the jaw parallel with the floor, and the back of the right hand should be resting in the left palm, with thumbs lightly touching. The meditator may sit on a cushion in order to facilitate a posture in which the spine is comfortably straight.

The practice generally begins with a confession, in which the meditator reflects on past transgressions and vows not to do them again. One then offers homage to all the buddhas and bodhisattvas and dedicates the merit gained through one's religious practice toward the welfare of all other sentient beings. Ideally the practice of Vajrasattva meditation should be combined with the mind of awakening, since one's ultimate goal should be attainment of buddhahood for the benefit of others.

With this mental preparation one is ready to begin the visualization practice. One first generates a mental image of a throne shaped like a lotus flower, with a cushion in the middle, and in the center of the disk is the syllable *hūṃ*. The *hūṃ* transforms into Vajrasattva, whose body is colored a luminous white. He is seated in the half-lotus posture, and the toe of his right foot rests on the head of the meditator. He has one face and two arms.[32] This mental image is often connected with guru yoga, and the meditator is instructed to imagine that Vajrasattva is his or her guru manifesting in a pure form.

Vajrasattva's right hand is at his heart and holds a golden vajra, while his left hand, at his waist, holds a bell with the hollow part facing upwards. These symbolize the key qualities toward which tantric meditators aspire: compassion and wisdom. The vajra is the symbol of wisdom united with skillful means, and the bell is the symbol of emptiness. He is wearing ornaments of precious jewels that adorn complete enjoyment bodies, and the *hūṃ* syllable is at his heart. The hundred-syllable mantra of Vajrasattva surrounds him in a counterclockwise direction, and the *hūṃ* radiates light in all directions. This light pervades all of space and benefits all sentient beings by removing their mental obstructions. It is crucial that the meditator also cultivate the understanding that the image is empty of inherent existence, completely insubstantial like a rainbow, a union of empty form and pure appearance. This is necessary because one should avoid reifying the image and becoming attached to it. The visualized Vajrasattva, like oneself, is a creation of mind and lacks true substantial existence.

Beginning meditators will be unable to get beyond the idea that this is a mental creation, but in advanced states of realization one understands that the image is one's own mind manifesting as Vajrasattva, who represents one's potential for awakening. It is neither more nor less real than the phenomena of ordinary experience, which are also manifestations of mind.

One now visualizes a stream of ambrosia (symbolizing the wisdom and compassion of Vajrasattva) issuing from the central syllables of the mantra,

32 This may seem obvious to people unfamiliar with the iconography of tantric deities, but many of them have multiple faces and arms.

entering through a hole at the top of one's head, and flowing downward through the body. As it descends, it displaces all of one's negative emotions, bad karmas, and mental afflictions, which are visualized as a dark, viscous substance that is expelled through the lower extremities, the pores of the skin, the palms of the hands, and the soles of the feet. In this way, all of one's negativities are replaced by the healing ambrosia, which permeates one's whole body and suffuses it with a sense of well-being.

After this initial purification, the meditator cultivates the feeling that her body has been transformed into that of Vajrasattva. The more convinced one is of this transformation, the more effective the meditation will be. One should dispel all sense of ordinariness and cultivate the idea that one has become Vajrasattva. One perceives oneself as having the body, speech, and mind of Vajrasattva, and one engages in the awakened activities of a buddha, acting spontaneously and effortlessly to benefit all sentient beings throughout space. In order to sustain this idea, one repeats Vajrasattva's hundred syllable mantra:

> *oṃ vajrasattva samayam anupālaya / vajrasattva tvenopatiṣṭha / dṛḍho me bhava / sutoṣyo me bhava / supośyo me bhava / anurakto me bhava/ sarva siddhiṃ me prayaccha / sarva karmasu ca me / citta śreyaḥ kuru / hūṃ ha ha ha ha hoḥ / bhagavan-sarva-tathāgata vajra mā me muñca vajrī bhava / mahāsamaya-sattva āḥ hūṃ /*

> *Oṃ* Vajrasattva, protect the pledge. Vajrasattva, may I be supported by you. Remain firmly with me; be pleased with me; be happy with me. Be affectionate toward me. Bestow all attainments on me. Purify my karma. Make my mind virtuous. *Hūṃ ha ha ha ha hoḥ*; all the blessed Tathāgatas, may I be liberated in the vajra, O great pledge being of the nature of the vajra, *aḥ hūṃ*.

In ngöndro practice, one repeats this mantra one hundred thousand times. It is often recommended that one also repeat the short Vajrasattva mantra, *oṃ vajrasattva hūṃ*. This should be done as often as possible, ideally six hundred thousand times. The purpose of this is to focus the mind on Vajrasattva and contemplate his function of mental purification. Through this one becomes increasingly familiar with the concept of purification, and this in turn contributes to its actualization within the psycho-physical continuum.

The meditator then recalls all past faults and transgressions of religious vows. She confesses them to Vajrasattva, asks for his blessings, and resolves not to commit such offenses in the future. Vajrasattva then dissolves into the meditator, and she contemplates the fact that this image, like her own psycho-physical continuum, is empty of inherent existence. She realizes that her own faults and negativities are similarly empty, void of substantial existence, and so they may be purified through appropriate practices.

At the end of every session of practice one offers any benefits that derive from it for the benefit of all sentient beings. This is an essential element of closure, since it assures that one's motivation is not a selfish one but that one is pursuing this practice due to altruistic intentions. In order to assure that one does not become attached to the form of the image, one then visualizes Vajrasattva being absorbed into light, and then he is absorbed into oneself. One thinks of one's own body, speech, and mind as being transformed into those of Vajrasattva, and one realizes that one has internalized the awakened qualities of the deity.

Maṇḍala Offering

As with the practice of prostration, maṇḍala offering involves physical activities conjoined with visualization. Practitioners making maṇḍala offerings imagine themselves giving valuable substances such as gold, jewels, etc. to buddhas and bodhisattvas, as well as the guru. Generally the ritual requires a base, which is a round plate about six inches in diameter. Ideally it should be made of gold, silver, or another precious metal, but in practice any surface may be used, even one made of stone or wood. No matter what the material is, the plate should be visualized as pure gold. This symbolizes the pure innate buddha nature of each person.

People of limited means often make offerings of grains or rice, and sometimes common stones, but those who can afford it may use precious gems. Other offerings may be added, such as coins, jewelry, etc. When grains are used, the practitioner begins by holding some in the left hand while holding the base at the level of the heart. With the right hand, he drops some grains into the center of the base while reciting the refuge prayer and attempting to generate the mind of awakening. With the right forearm, he wipes the grain off the base in a clockwise direction. This symbolizes the removal of the three afflictions of desire, hatred, and ignorance, which obscure the innate buddha nature. The right arm is used because an energy channel associated with wisdom runs along it.

Next the practitioner drops some grains on the base and wipes it three times in a counterclockwise direction. This is symbolic of the wish to develop the exalted qualities of the body, speech, and mind of a buddha.

The succeeding stage involves pouring grain in the hand and then into the center of the base. One then makes a fence around the perimeter by pouring more grain in a clockwise direction. After this, a hill of grain is formed in the middle, symbolizing Mount Meru, the center of the universe in traditional Buddhist cosmology. Around it are piles of grain representing the four primary continents described in traditional Buddhist literature, one at each of the cardinal points. One then makes two more piles on either side of the central one, which correspond to the sun and moon. While creating this maṇḍala, the practitioner should be creatively visualizing it as containing the entire universe and all its desirable things. The universe in the form of the maṇḍala is then given to the buddhas while one recites a prayer of offering.

After the prayer has been recited and one has imagined oneself giving everything in the universe to the buddhas, one tilts the maṇḍala toward oneself and pours the grains into one's lap, imagining that the buddhas reciprocate by bestowing blessings. This practice is said to be an effective way of generating merit and of overcoming attachment to material things. By symbolically proffering everything imaginable to the buddhas for the benefit of all sentient beings, one diminishes one's desire for wealth and possessions. As with the practice of prostrations, it is customary for practitioners to perform this at least one hundred thousand times.

Guru Yoga

All schools of Tibetan Buddhism emphasize the necessity of finding a qualified teacher. Such a teacher is one who has successfully traversed the path and attained the highest levels of realization. Because of this, the guru can guide students around the pitfalls they will encounter, warn them of dangers, correct their errors, and skillfully help them to actualize their potential buddhahood. It is stated throughout Tibetan meditation literature that one cannot successfully follow the path of tantra without a guru.

Guru yoga purifies one's awareness through practices that involve visualizing the teacher as an embodiment of the pure, exalted wisdom of buddhahood. Unlike a deity mentally generated in front of one, arising from emptiness and again dissolved into emptiness at the end of the session, the guru remains with one as a symbol of the goal of awakening. The guru transmits Buddhist teachings, instructs us on their proper application, and provides an example of a person who puts them into practice.

Imagining one's guru as a buddha provides a concrete example of the awakened state one is trying to achieve. Successful Vajrayāna practice requires the ability to see the guru as a buddha and to understand that any apparent faults the guru might have are only reflections of one's own inadequacies. The guru is a reflection of one's own mind, and a meditator who perceives the guru as having faults develops corresponding flaws. One who views the guru as a buddha actualizes the innate potential for buddhahood in each sentient being.

Lineage

In addition to providing meditators with living examples of realized beings, gurus also belong to lineages of teachings and practices that are traced back to the beginnings of Buddhism. The lineage is a guarantee of the authenticity of the teachings. Tibetan Buddhism is a traditional system, and its leaders are revered not for their innovations but for how closely they approximate its ideals. Great teachers and adepts are presented in Tibetan literature as archetypal models, and their biographies tend to stress the ways in which they embody the shared values of the tradition.

In keeping with these attitudes, gurus are important because they belong to established lineages, and students who receive initiation from a guru are told of the succession of awakened teachers who have passed on that particular teaching. This is partly due to a respect for precedent and a backward-looking orientation found in all traditional systems, but it is also a recognition that Vajrayāna is not transmitted primarily through texts and scriptures, but from mind to mind, from teacher to student. Gurus do not simply learn the texts and practice the relevant meditations: they also receive a rich oral heritage from their own teachers, and each successive generation augments this legacy, while striving to retain a perceived connection with the past.

This oral transmission is essential for newly initiated students to enter into the system at all, since many tantric texts are deliberately cryptic. Tantric teachings are secret, and the texts assume that their words will be explained by a qualified master who has studied and internalized Vajrayāna lore from his or her own teachers and whose meditation has led to advanced states of spiritual development. The ideal guru is a person who is firmly rooted in the tradition, who has studied the texts and commentaries extensively, who has deeply internalized oral instructions from awakened masters, and who has put the teachings into practice in meditation.

Tantric texts also emphasize that the guru should be a person whose meditations have borne fruit, since only those who have purified their own mental continuums are able to perceive the spiritual defects and needs of others and adapt their teachings to them. Such a person provides students with a model to emulate, a once-ordinary being like themselves who through meditative practice has become extraordinary. Role models of awakened behavior are essential in order for beginners to be able to imagine themselves as awakened masters embodying wisdom and compassion, working ceaselessly for the benefit of others.

It is important to note, however, that the purpose of exalting the guru is not to give praise to one's teacher. An awakened being has no need for praise and is unaffected by censure. Gurus are extolled and visualized as deities in order to enhance one's own spiritual practice. Learning to perceive an apparently ordinary being as a deity helps people to overcome their attachments to feelings of ordinariness, to transform the mundane through creative visualization. Through this practice, one learns to overcome one's own limitations and to recast the world in accordance with the symbols and practices of tantra.

Death and Dying in Tibetan Buddhism

Tibetan Buddhism places a particularly strong emphasis on instructions concerning death, and Tibetan literature contains numerous admonitions to be aware of the inevitability of death, the preciousness of the opportunities that a human birth presents, and the great value of mindfulness of death. A person who correctly grasps the inevitability of death becomes more focused on religious practice, since he or she realizes that death is inevitable, the time of death is uncertain, and so every moment counts.

An example of this attitude can be found in the biography of Milarépa, who began his meditative practice after having killed a number of people through black magic. The realization of his impending death and the sufferings he would experience in his next lifetime prompted him to find a lama who could show him a way to avert his fate. His concern with death was so great that when he was meditating in a cave his tattered clothes fell apart, but he decided not to mend them, saying, "If I were to die this evening, it would be wiser to meditate than to do this useless sewing."[33]

This attitude epitomizes the ideal for a Buddhist practitioner, according to many teachers. Atiśa, the Indian master who played a major role in the revival of Buddhism in Tibet in the eleventh century, is said to have told his students that for a person who is unaware of death, meditation has little power, but a person who is mindful of death and impermanence progresses steadily and makes the most of every precious moment. A famous saying of the school he founded, the Kadampa, holds that if one does not meditate on death in the morning, the whole morning is wasted; if one does not meditate on death at noon, the afternoon is wasted; and if one does not meditate on death at night, the evening is wasted.

Using the Death Process to Advantage

In tantric systems, death is portrayed as an opportunity for spiritual progress and not simply as a limiting condition that represents the termination of life. One applies generation stage yogas to the death process, using the procedure of "taking the three bodies as the path." This involves perceiving the clear light of death as the truth body, the intermediate state between death and rebirth (*bar do*) as the complete enjoyment body, and the rebirth process as the emanation body.[34]

33 See Lobsang Lhalungpa, tr., *The Life of Milarepa* (New York: Arkana, 1984), p. 119.

34 Chapter 2, "Mahāyāna," discusses the "three bodies."

In the first method, one realizes that the truth body is of the nature of one's own mind, which is a union of clear light and emptiness. A person who successfully cultivates this understanding transforms the clear light nature of the mind into the truth body, thus quickly actualizing the state of buddhahood.

Perceiving the bardo state as the complete enjoyment body involves taking control of the bardo process. After death one enters the intermediate state, in which one is confronted by powerful images and other sensations. Intermediate state yogas develop the ability to direct the manifestations and contents of the visions of the bardo, rather than being helplessly moved along through the process. One learns that all perceptions are creations of mind, and a person who becomes skilled in this practice develops the conscious ability to direct the production of mental images. Most beings in the bardo are assaulted by strange and unnerving sights, sounds, and smells, but the experienced meditator understands that they are creations of mind. After realizing this and learning to exercise control over the process of emanation, the meditator works at developing the level of skill necessary to visualize herself as a complete enjoyment body.

Perceiving the rebirth process as the emanation body is founded on the same principles as the previous two practices. In this technique the meditator develops awareness that a buddha's ability to produce emanation bodies is an extension of the sort of control that advanced meditators gain in creating mental images that appear to be real but are produced from emptiness. The process of rebirth can be influenced by a person who attains the mental discipline required for advanced visualization. Thus, one need not be thrown helplessly toward the next birth, and a yogin who becomes skilled in taking control over the rebirth process can develop the ability to determine the sort of life situation into which she will be born.

When a person dies naturally (that is, when death is not a result of a violent act or sudden accident), the various aspects of the psycho-physical continuum begin to disintegrate. At each stage in this process, one of the body's constituent elements dissolves and a particular mind emerges. This process continues through the time at which circulation and respiration stop. This is the point at which Western medicine considers a person to be dead, but according to Tibetan physiology and meditation theory, actual death has not yet occurred. Consciousness still inhabits the body, and until it departs one is not considered to be truly dead, although to all outward appearances this is the case.

The Internal Process of Death according to Tantric Theory

The bardo state has many pitfalls that trap the unwary and lead to future pain and suffering. Fortunately, there are ways to prepare for the dangers and increase one's chances of being able to take advantage of the opportunities afforded by the bardo. Among the most effective of these are yogic practices that simulate the process of death. A person who becomes familiar with these is not shocked or terrified by what he experiences in the bardo, but rather recognizes everything as images created by the mind. A meditator who has developed proficiency in the yogic practices of the bardo is also less likely to become terrified by the process of physical and mental degeneration that precedes death. Understanding the stages of death and the physiological reasons that underlie them enhances one's ability to remain calm during the process, and this can also help one to recognize the events of the bardo for what they are.

The yogas of bardo preparation are based on simulating death. They are founded on the mystical physiology of Vajrayāna that describes the human body in terms of winds and channels through which the winds travel. According to this system, death is the result of the progressive collapse of the ability of the winds to act as supports for consciousness. When they are no longer able to perform this function, death occurs.

When a person dies, the winds that are the bases of consciousness dissolve into the right and left channels. These then dissolve into the wind in the central channel, causing a loosening of the pressure exerted on the central channel by the right and left channels at the cakras. This allows a freer movement of wind in the central channel, which leads to the manifestation of subtle minds.

These minds are always present but are normally submerged beneath the coarser levels of consciousness; these coarser minds are what ordinary beings experience most of the time. When the restrictions are loosened, however, the more subtle minds manifest, which presents a valuable opportunity to work with them in a meditative context. Unfortunately, most people do not realize this opportunity for what it is, and instead react with fear, since they feel that they are being annihilated. Practitioners of highest yoga tantra should recognize these subtle minds and understand that there is in fact no "I" that can be threatened with annihilation. Adepts can take advantage of the arising of the subtle minds and manipulate them in accordance with the goals of tantric practice.

At each of the cakras are red and white "drops," which are bases for mental health. The white drops are more numerous at the top of the head, while the red drops are more common at the solar plexus. The origins of these drops are the white and red substances one inherits from one's father and mother, respectively. At the time of conception, white matter from the father's sperm and red matter from the mother's ovum form the nucleus of the zygote, and the matter one receives from them at conception resides at the heart in what is called the "indestructible drop," which is the size of a small pea. It is white at the top and red at the bottom, and it is called "indestructible" because it remains until death. The subtle life-sustaining winds reside in it, and when one dies all winds dissolve into it. After it has absorbed all winds, the clear light of death becomes manifest.

According to tantric theory, the residence of the mind is not the brain, but the heart. The mind abides in the indestructible drop at the heart cakra. There are two types of indestructible drop, one coarse and one subtle. The coarse drop is a coalescence of cells from the semen of the father and the ovum of the mother, and the subtle drop is a coalescence of subtle levels of consciousness and subtle physical energies. The coarse drop is "indestructible" because it endures throughout one's life, from the moment of conception until the final moment of physical death. The subtle drop is "indestructible" because it endures throughout all of one's lives, from beginningless time and into the future, until the time of awakening, at which point one's body is transformed into the perfect body of a buddha.

When the vital energies that sustain life break down, the dying person experiences a reversal of the process of conception that initiated his life. According to Tibetan medical theory, during one's life the cells that came from one's father and the cells that came from one's mother (both of which joined at conception) separate and subsequently reside in different parts of the body. The cells of the original sperm from one's father are located at the cakra at the top of the head during one's life, and the cells from the mother's ovum are at the navel cakra. Throughout one's life, these are kept separate by the vital energies in the body, particularly those in the central channel. As one's energy fades, however, the vital energies are no longer sufficient to separate these two sets of cells, and they begin to move from the cakras where they were stored.

The white cells of the father's sperm move downward from the crown cakra through the central channel until they come to the heart. While they are moving, one experiences a vision of snowlike whiteness as they travel through the cakras. Then the cells of the mother's ovum move upward toward the heart, where the two types of cells meet. At this point the dying person has a vision of darkness similar to a sky that is completely covered with dark clouds.

People who have not meditated in advance of this faint when the vision appears, but skilled meditators recognize what is happening and remain conscious. This is a particularly potent opportunity for meditative progress, since the grosser levels of mind are dropping away, making access to subtle consciousnesses easier.

Physically, the body continues to degenerate, and eventually the heart gives a slight tremble, which signifies that consciousness has left the body. One experiences a vision of clear light that is like dawn breaking in a cloudless sky. This is termed the "clear light of death," and according to Tibetan medical literature this is the actual point of death.

Ordinary people undergoing these changes are terrified. Tantric yogins, however, prepare for them during their lifetimes and simulate the process of death in meditation, and so they are untroubled by these experiences. A person who has practiced preparatory yogas and used them to gain control over the mind can use the death process to great advantage, since it presents a tremendous opportunity for spiritual progress.

The most important trainings involve gaining control over the vital energies and recognizing the subtler levels of consciousness. A meditator who becomes skilled in the practices of highest yoga tantra learns to influence the movements of subtle energies and gains access to the subtler levels of consciousness, and so when the coarse energies dissolve into the subtler ones and grosser levels of mind dissolve into the subtler ones, he is not surprised. One who has simulated this process during life is well prepared for death, and when the images and sensations of the bardo appear, he will recognize them as products of the mind, which can be influenced and manipulated in accordance with a yogin's wishes in order to produce particular soteriological results.

Influencing the Death Process

A skilled tantric practitioner who takes control over the process of death is able to transform the subtle energies and consciousnesses into the bodies of a buddha. Consciousness is transmuted into the truth body, wisdom and energy into the complete enjoyment body, the clear light of death arises as the truth body, and the visions of the bardo are transformed into emanation bodies.

When the mind of clear light manifests, one experiences it as a completely nondualistic voidness. It is the subtlest and most fundamental level of consciousness. A person who is proficient in generation-stage yogas can take advantage of this extremely subtle level of mind and transmute the light into the truth body. Yogins who successfully merge the clear light into the truth body instantaneously attain buddhahood and pass through the bardo.

The Bardo Process

After the mind of clear light dawns, people generally remain in this state of lucidity for three days, but most are so frightened by the strangeness of the experience that they lapse into unconsciousness, unaware of what is happening. At the end of this stage, external signs of death appear, such as pus or blood emerging from the nose and sexual organ. This indicates that consciousness has departed from the body, and only at this point should the corpse be disposed of. Before this time, consciousness is still in the body, and if it is handled violently, buried, or cremated, this could negatively influence the consciousness of the dying person, possibly resulting in a lower rebirth.

Since the body and mind are no longer able to sustain life, this is the end of one's life and the beginning of an interim existence in the bardo. After the clear light ceases, the previous process of manifestation of progressively subtler minds is reversed, and one is born into the bardo.[35]

35 The classic work on this subject is entitled *Liberation through Hearing in the Intermediate*

At this point one acquires a subtle body that accords with one's future rebirth. If one is to be reborn as a human, one will have a bardo body that is human in appearance; if one is to be reborn as an animal, one's bardo body will resemble the type of animal one will become, and so forth. The bardo body is unhampered by physical restrictions and can travel wherever one wills and can pass through walls and other physical objects. This state can last from a moment up to seven days. If one either averts rebirth through yogic practice or is unable to locate a suitable rebirth situation, one undergoes a "small death" in which one experiences the death sequence outlined earlier, but this time it happens very quickly. Then the rebirth process is repeated, and one takes a second birth in the bardo, with a new bardo body. This can happen as many as seven times, making a total of forty-nine days in which one may be in the bardo. After this one must find a place of rebirth.

Trainees of highest capacity who are prepared for the bardo and have developed proficiency in generation stage yogas can manifest the clear light of death as a tantric deity in accordance with a tantric system (e.g., Guhyasamāja, Cakrasaṃvara, etc.). A person who accomplishes this bypasses the bardo altogether and arises in the form of a tantric deity, endowed with all the outer and inner signs of perfection. This is a result of previous successful simulation of the process of death and training in tantric yogas. A person who becomes adept in these practices realizes that all appearances are creations of mind and that mind itself is a union of clear luminosity and emptiness. The yogas of the bardo begin with this insight, and the meditator transforms the clear light nature of the mind into the fully awakened mind of a buddha and the vital energies into a buddha's subtle body.

Those who are not advanced enough to accomplish this, but who have gained a measure of control over the vital energies, have other options. If one is able to recognize the stages of the process of dissolution of vital energies, when the coarse elements dissolve and the clear light of death manifests, one can generate the clear light of death into the "clear light of the path," thus making the nature of the mind indistinguishable from the path. This is called "merging the mother and son clear light."

State (*Bar do thos grol*), attributed to Padmasambhava and discovered by the famed "discoverer of secret treasures" (*gter ston*) Karma Lingpa (c. fourteenth century).

Taking Rebirth

At the end of the bardo process, one is drawn toward a rebirth appropriate to one's future life situation. Ordinary beings rush heedlessly toward their own suffering, not realizing the pitfalls their attitudes create for them. Feelings of desire, anger, resentment, etc. create the connection between lives and are responsible for making the final move from the bardo state to a new life. As long as one has such mental afflictions, one will continue to be reborn helplessly, pushed along by past actions and dispositions. Until one breaks this vicious cycle, one is like a prisoner: there is some possibility for movement in many cases, but one is still trapped by one's previous karma.

6: The Four Orders

Similarities and Differences

Among adherents of the four main orders of Tibetan Buddhism—Nyingma, Kagyu, Sakya, and Géluk—there is a tendency to emphasize the differences that distinguish them, but much more striking is how much they share in common. All stress common themes, such as the importance of overcoming attachment to the phenomena of cyclic existence and the idea that it is necessary for trainees to develop an attitude of sincere renunciation. Another important point of agreement lies in rules of monastic discipline: all orders of Tibetan Buddhism follow the vinaya of the Mūlasarvāstivāda school, which has been the standard in Tibetan monasteries since the founding of the first monastic institution at Samyé. In addition, they also share the same corpus of philosophical and liturgical texts imported from India, and all four orders present a path to awakening that incorporates practices of sūtra and tantra systems.

They also share some common assumptions about the doctrines and practices they inherited from India. It is generally agreed that the Buddha provided divergent dispensations for various types of trainees, and these have been codified by Tibetan doxographers, who categorize Buddha's teachings in terms of three distinct vehicles—the Lesser Vehicle (Hīnayāna), the Great Vehicle (Mahāyāna), and the Vajra Vehicle (Vajrayāna)—each of which was intended to appeal to the spiritual capacities of particular groups.

All four Tibetan orders agree on the basic outline of the path one should follow to escape from cyclic existence and the sorts of practices that one should adopt. All share a Mahāyāna orientation, and so they agree that the path begins with the generation of the mind of awakening and progresses through the bodhisattva levels, during which one cultivates the six (or ten) perfections. It is assumed by members of the four orders that Vajrayāna is the supreme of all Buddhist paths, although there are differences between them regarding which tantras they favor and which lineages they follow. The Nyingma order, for instance, emphasizes the "great perfection" (*rdzogs chen;* pronounced "dzogchen"), and its tantric practices are mainly based on the so-called "Old Tantras" (such as the *Secret Basic Essence Tantra*) and on instructions found in "hidden treasures" (*gter ma;* pronounced "terma"). The Kagyupas emphasize the *mahāmudrā* system inherited from the Indian master Tilopa, and its tantric practices are mainly derived from the *Guhyasamāja Tantra* and the *Cakrasaṃvara Tantra*. The Gélukpa system of tantric theory and practice is based on the *Guhyasamāja Tantra*, the *Cakrasaṃvara Tantra*, and the *Kālacakra Tantra*. The Sakyapas favor the *Hevajra Tantra*, which is the basis of their "path and result" (*lam 'bras;* pronounced "lamdré") system.

Each order traces its lineage to particular Indian masters. There are distinctive differences in their actual tantric practices, but despite these differences there are many points of commonality. This has been noted by the Dalai Lama, who states that the philosophical view of all orders is that of the Middle Way School of Nāgārjuna, and in terms of practice all follow the program of Mahāyāna. In addition, their paths and tenets incorporate the systems of the sūtras and tantras in their entirety, and so he concludes that all of them are equally effective programs for bringing sentient beings to liberation.[36]

If one compares the four orders of Tibetan Buddhism to Theravāda Buddhism, or to Chinese, Japanese, or Korean schools, the disparities are more pronounced. This is a result of important differences in their respective histories of transmission of Buddhism, and the style of practice and teaching in each country is reflective of this history, as well as cultural and linguistic factors and subsequent political and religious developments.

Tibetan Buddhists share a common heritage that came to them from the scholastic institutions of northern India during the period of the dissemination of Buddhism to Tibet and tantric lineages that mainly centered

36 Tenzin Gyatso, H.H. the Fourteenth Dalai Lama, "Talk of His Holiness the Dalai Lama at the Nyingma Institute," *Gesar* 6.3 (1980), p. 4.

in Bihar and Bengal, combined with cultural factors that influenced later developments. Many of the influential masters who came to Tibet viewed Vajrayāna as the supreme of all Buddhist teachings and practices, and so it is not surprising that Tibetan Buddhism also regards it in this way.

In Tibet, the dominant form of religious practice is the tantric Buddhism inherited from India, and there is also a high degree of compatibility in the philosophical views of the four orders. Particularly important is their agreement on the nature of the mind, since mental training is the focus of the Buddhist path as practiced in Tibet. All four orders agree that the mind is of the nature of clear light. All posit various levels of consciousness that are differentiated in terms of relative coarseness or subtlety, and all agree that the most subtle and basic level of mind is of the nature of pure luminosity and emptiness.

In the practices of highest yoga tantra that are found in the New Translation orders,[37] one cultivates the awareness that the mind is of a nature of luminosity and bliss and that all mental defilements are adventitious and not a part of the nature of mind. The same is true of the *dzogchen* system (the supreme teaching in the Nyingma order), which takes this insight as the key element of its program of meditative training. In both systems, one learns to view phenomena as the creative sport of mind, and thoughts are perceived as arising from emptiness and again merging into emptiness.

Each order has its own distinctive ways of leading trainees toward buddhahood, and each has developed characteristic styles and terminology, but all of them share fundamental assumptions about the path and about Buddhist doctrine. More importantly, as the Dalai Lama argues, all can demonstrate that their methods have succeeded in producing outstanding meditators who embody the highest ideals of Tibetan Buddhism and whose lives and teachings stand as testaments to the effectiveness of the systems of each of the four orders.

37 The New Translation orders are Kagyu, Sakya, and Géluk, who base their philosophical systems and practices on the translations that were prepared according to the rules and standards developed during the period of the second dissemination of Buddhism into Tibet. The "old translations" are those prepared during the first dissemination, which began with the arrival of Padmasambhava and Śāntarakṣita in Tibet. These are favored by the Nyingma order.

The Nonsectarian Movement

In spite of the many similarities in view and practice among the traditions of Tibetan Buddhism, sectarian controversy has been a recurring feature in Tibet since earliest times. Every order has produced scathing attacks on its perceived rivals, and the history of Tibetan Buddhism is marked by oral debates between competing groups as well as persecutions and factional wars. In the late nineteenth century, several prominent lamas in eastern Tibet began a countermovement, commonly referred to as "Nonsectarian" (*Ris med*; pronounced "Rimé"). It was a direct challenge to the scholastic approach of the Gélukpa order, whose educational system mainly relies on textbooks that summarize key philosophical and doctrinal points. The definitions (*mtshan nyid*) they contain are derived from Indian "root texts" (including sūtras, philosophical treatises, and tantras); these are memorized by students and form the basis of their curriculum and examinations.

The Nonsectarian lamas, by contrast, required their students to study Indian sūtras and philosophical texts, and much of the Nonsectarian literature consists of original commentaries on them. The philosophical basis of most Nonsectarian lamas is the "other-emptiness" (*gzhan stong*) view, which posits a self-existent ultimate reality that can only be understood by direct meditative perception. Another important aspect of Rimé is the vision of the great perfection developed by the "treasure discoverer" (*gter ston*) Jikmé Lingpa (1730-1798). His revelation of the *Innermost Essence of the Great Expanse* cycle of practice is one of the foundational sources of the movement.

His reincarnation Jamyang Khyentsé Ongbo (1820-1892) became one of the leading figures in the Nonsectarian movement. Like other Nonsectarian lamas, he advocated a universalist approach to Buddhist teachings, according to which all were said to have value for particular practitioners. Students were encouraged to study extensively in various traditions, and as Gene Smith has pointed out, one of the key features of the movement was an encyclopedic orientation.[38] Nonsectarian lamas produced a num-

38 E. Gene Smith, *Among Tibetan Texts: History and Literature of the Himalayan Plateau* (Boston: Wisdom Publications, 2001), pp. 227–272. The term *Rimé* is sometimes rendered as "eclectic" by contemporary scholars, but the products and teachings of this tradition indicate that this is inappropriate. David Seyfort Ruegg points out that *Rimé* is more encyclopedic or

ber of compendia of Buddhist learning, most notably Jamgön Kongtrül's (1813–1899) *Compendium of All Knowledge*. Unlike some scholars of his time, who focused on certain works they regarded as normative and rejected others, Kongtrül and his students traveled throughout Tibet searching for texts, initiations, and oral lineages—both those that were widely popular and others that were obscure and local—and brought them together in huge collections. Contrary to those who claimed that one approach is superior to all others, they sought to make available as many teachings and practices as possible so that students could choose those that were most effective. Their sources were not limited to religious or philosophical texts, and they incorporated folk traditions and popular literature, including such classics as the *Epic of Gésar of Ling*.

By contrast, the Gélukpa scholars of the time tended to reiterate the paradigms that had been handed down to them and engage in rote and unoriginal scholarship. There were some notable and original scholars among the Gélukpas, but the main monasteries of the order were generally bastions of dogmatic conservatism, and authors of the time mainly composed textbooks that elaborated on definitions and debates found in earlier texts. Many of these laid out possible debates and counterarguments in great detail, and these were memorized by students. They provided set refutations against potential opponents, and so students simply learned to identify a mistaken view and apply the appropriate label, rather than examining philosophical positions on their own merits. The Rimé masters, however, urged their students to look at the Indic root texts and to take in the oral instructions of a variety of teachers in order that they would become acquainted with a range of perspectives. The emphasis was on direct understanding rather than repetition of established "correct" positions.

In keeping with its nondogmatic approach, the Nonsectarian movement was not a distinct school with fixed doctrines, nor did it create a distinctive monastic order with its own institutions. Instead, its proponents maintained allegiance to their own lineages but adopted elements from the various Buddhist traditions available to them.

---

universalistic than eclectic. *Ris med* is the antonym of *ris su chad pa*, and so it has connotations of being unbounded, all-embracing, and impartial ("A Tibetan's Odyssey: A Review Article," *Journal of the Royal Asiatic Society* 2 [1989], p. 310).

Like Jikmé Lingpa, many of the great Rimé masters came from non-aristocratic backgrounds and generally shunned institutional Buddhism. Because of the emphasis on lineage, there is generally a particularly close bond between lamas and students. Retreats are a core element of the tradition, and students are often guided by their teachers for extended periods of practice in solitude. The literature of Rimé emphasizes the beneficial results of long retreats and the importance of regular engagement in solitary meditation. Not surprisingly given this emphasis, biographies of the luminaries of the tradition emphasize visions, trances, revelations, and oral instructions. Many of the prominent Nonsectarian lamas were also treasure discoverers, and disclosures of new "hidden treasures" are an important aspect of its history.

Most contemporary lamas of the non-Gélukpa traditions are directly influenced by this important movement, and many of its practices have also found their way into the Gélukpa order. One key difference between Nonsectarian traditions and the Gélukpas is the doctrine of other-emptiness, which is a cornerstone of most Rimé practice but is staunchly rejected by the Gélukpas. (Not all Rimé masters hold to this view, however; Mipam is a prominent example of a Rimé lama who like the Gélukpas adhered to the self-emptiness view.)

Other-Emptiness

As we have seen, the doctrine of emptiness figures prominently in Indian and Tibetan Buddhist thought. Questions regarding how emptiness should be interpreted have been a major source of debate between the various orders of Tibetan Buddhism, and they continue to generate controversy today.

The two most influential factions advocate, respectively, the doctrines of "other-emptiness" (*gzhan stong*; pronounced "shendong") and "self-emptiness" (rang stong; pronounced "rangdong"). The latter position is held by the Gélukpa order, which follows the interpretation of Madhyamaka developed by Tsong Khapa. He contended that emptiness is a "nonaffirming negative," meaning that it is simply a radical denial of inherent existence (*rang bzhin, svabhāva*), a quality falsely attributed to phenomena by ordinary beings. From the perspective of an ignorant consciousness, phenomena appear to exist by themselves and are not viewed as composites of smaller parts created by causes and conditions and subject to decay, and persons appear to possess enduring selves that are independent of the vicissitudes of birth, death, and change. The Gélukpas deny that there is any enduring substance and hold that all phenomena are collections of parts that are constantly changing due to the influence of causes and conditions.

According to the other-emptiness interpretation, emptiness is the ultimate truth and is conceived as a self-existent, unchanging reality that pervades all phenomena. It is empty of what is other than itself, that is, the mistaken perceptions attributed to it by deluded beings. But it is not void of itself, since it is the final nature of all phenomena. The emptiness of the Gélukpas is said to be "dead emptiness" (*bem stong*) because it would be a state devoid of any qualities. Proponents of other-emptiness claim that it is in fact the repository of all the qualities of buddhahood and is inherent in all beings. It cannot be known by logic or conceptuality and is only realized by advanced yogins through direct, nonconceptual insight. The Gélukpas denounce this position as an attempt to reify the Absolute and smuggle Indian substantialist notions into Buddhism.

One of the key debates between the Gélukpas and their opponents who advocate the other-emptiness position concerns how the doctrine of the "womb of the *tathāgata*" (*de bzhin gzhegs pa'i snying po*, *tathāgata-garbha*) should be understood. This notion, found in some Indian Buddhist texts, holds that all sentient beings have the potential to become buddhas. Advocates of other-emptiness conceive of this potential as a positive, self-existent essence that pervades all existence and is made manifest through meditative training but is not created by it.

Buddhahood is the basic nature of mind, and it is subtle, ineffable, and beyond the grasp of conceptual thought. It cannot be described in words and can only be understood through direct experience. According to this position, all phenomena are of the nature of mind, which is a union of luminosity and emptiness. They have no substantial existence and merely exist within the continuum of mind. Initiations by Rimé masters—particularly those who belong to the Nyingma and Kagyu orders, which emphasize the formless meditations of the great completion and great seal, respectively—commonly feature oral instructions in which lamas "point out the nature of mind" to students, who are then instructed to cultivate a direct apprehension of this reality themselves. Those who succeed in grasping the nature of mind and perceiving all phenomena as emanations of luminosity and emptiness are able to attain buddhahood in a single instant of awakening.

The Gélukpas follow the Indian gradualist tradition, which holds that the path to buddhahood consists in progressively perfecting the matrix of good qualities that characterize awakened beings. This is accomplished during many lifetimes of arduous training, during which meditators follow a step-by-step approach and progressively rid themselves of negative propensities while simultaneously acquiring deeper insight and qualities like generosity, ethics, and patience, which they did not have when they began the path. According to this interpretation, *tathāgata-garbha* should be understood as being equivalent to emptiness, conceived as a nonaffirming negative. It is another way of expressing the idea that beings lack any enduring essence, and so they have the ability to effect changes in their psycho-physical continuums. If they choose to follow the Buddhist path, they can move toward buddhahood because there is no self, soul, or essence that endures from moment to moment.

Nyingma

The Nyingma order has the longest established history of transmission of all the four major traditions of Tibetan Buddhism. This is reflected in the name "Nyingma," which literally means "Old Order." The other three main schools of Tibetan Buddhism—Sakya, Kagyu, and Géluk—are collectively referred to as Sarma (*gSar ma*), or "New Orders," because they rely on the Tibetan translations of Indian Buddhist texts that were prepared under the system established during the second dissemination of Buddhism.

Nyingma primarily relies on the old translations, particularly of tantric texts, and its Tibetan origins are traced to Buddhist pioneers of the time of Tibet's imperial dynasty (ca. seventh-ninth centuries).

According to Nyingma lineage histories, the original teacher of the doctrines that came to be associated with the Old Order was Samantabhadra, who is the "primordial buddha" and who embodies the truth body of all buddhas. Nyingma also identifies Vajradhara (an emanation of Samantabhadra) and the buddhas of the five buddha families as the original promulgators of many of its teachings and practices. These are complete enjoyment bodies, whose teachings are primarily adapted to the cognitive capacities of very advanced practitioners.

In addition to these figures, this lineage also has a succession of distinguished human teachers, the most important of whom is Padmasambhava, who according to traditional histories played a decisive role in the first transmission of Buddhism to Tibet. Because of their strong links to Padmasambhava—as well as other eminent first-dissemination teachers like Vimalamitra, Vairocana, and Śāntarakṣita—the Nyingmapas feel that their lineage represents the most authentic and complete teachings of the early masters who brought Buddhism to the Land of Snows. Nyingma tradition contains a complex array of intersecting lineages, including lineages of transmission of vinaya teachings and practices, sūtras, tantras, "hidden treasures" (*terma*), etc. Of crucial importance for Nyingma masters is the "teaching" (*bka' ma*) tradition, which begins with Samantabhadra and consists of doctrines, texts, practices, rituals, and realizations that have been passed on from master to disciple in an unbroken chain.

Padmasambhava

By far the most influential of Nyingma teachers is Padmasambhava—known to Tibetans as "Guru Rinpoché"—who probably lived during the eighth century C.E. Traditional histories report that his missionary work spread the lineage into Tibet. He is regarded by Nyingmapas as an emanation of the buddha Amitābha whose particular goal was to facilitate the dissemination of Buddhism in the crucial early period.

Although later histories present him as a towering figure in the early spread of Buddhism and credit him with wondrous magical abilities, in the ancient records he is a minor figure. The earliest mention of him, in the *Statement of Ba,* only briefly alludes to him as an itinerant Indian water-diviner and does not accord him any role in the propagation of Buddhism.

Terma: Hidden Treasures

The fortunes and developments of the New Orders are often closely connected with political and social factors, and all of them to a greater or lesser extent became involved in Tibetan politics. The Nyingma order, by contrast, has remained remarkably aloof from political intrigues. One result of this orientation, however, was that the tradition at times became insular and detached from current events. Nyingma histories report that the early teachers of the lineage had foreseen this problem, and they created the institution of hiding texts and artifacts that would be discovered at a later date and would breathe new life into the tradition. These "hidden treasures" are said to be secreted throughout the land of Tibet, and they are safeguarded by spells that prevent them from being found before the appropriate time.[39] When conditions are ripe for their dissemination, the terma are discovered by *tertön* (*gter ston*), or "treasure discoverers." These people are prophesied by the masters who hid the treasures, and there are strict controls and tests regarding the finding and propagation of terma. Many of the most influential treasures are texts, but others are religious objects.

Historically the most influential terma have been the "eight Heruka sādhanas" (liturgical cycles) and the *Innermost Essence of the Great Expanse*, which were hidden by Padmasambhava. Anticipating a time in which they would be needed, he concealed them, predicting the occasion of their discovery and the people who would find them. Other texts were secreted by his consort Yéshé Tsogyel, who memorized his teachings and then hid them with the help of Padmasambhava. Although later Nyingma tradition tends to emphasize Padmasambhava and his disciples as the sole proprietors of hidden treasures, the earliest ones were attributed to the dharma kings Songtsen Gambo and Tri Songdétsen.

According to the tradition, treasure discoverers are bodhisattvas who possess special qualities that enable them to find terma. When the time comes for a terma to be discovered, the discoverer finds a secret "hint" or "key" (*kha byung* or *lde mig*) that indicates the place of concealment. The great tertöns are emanations of Padmasambhava whose primary purpose is to locate the appropriate treasure at the appropriate time. In addition,

39 The terma have an ambiguous status in Tibetan Buddhism. They are generally associated with the Nyingma and Kagyu orders, but there have also been Géluk and Sakya treasure discoverers, and some of these texts are part of the paracanonical literature of all four orders. There has been considerable debate, however, regarding the authenticity of certain terma. Early terma are claimed to have been hidden by figures from the early dynastic period, and later most terma were attributed to Padmasambhava or his disciples. Many contain "prophecies" that purport to predict future events, but the texts appear to have been "discovered" well after the predicted events occurred, which has fueled suspicions regarding their provenance. Some opponents view the tradition of hidden treasures as a device to put a veneer of antiquity on new doctrines and practices, but the Nyingmapas staunchly defend the validity of their main terma.

each tertön is specially qualified to explain and transmit the terma he or she finds.

This system has proven effective in regularly breathing new life into the Nyingma order while maintaining a perceived link with its origins. Each age finds the terma appropriate to its spiritual needs, and each new terma becomes a part of the tradition. A number of Nyingma monasteries were founded to preserve and transmit these revelations, which facilitated their institutionalization. This, in turn, helped the recipients of this lore to develop the sort of structures that could guarantee its continued survival through the vicissitudes of Tibetan history.

The hidden treasures are often written in a code called "ḍākinī language" that can only be deciphered by people who have been taught how to read it. Ḍākinīs commonly aid in the process of discovery and in interpreting the terma. There are numerous safeguards that prevent terma being discovered before the appropriate time, including a "time-lock formula" (*gtsug las khan*). This ensures that only the ordained discoverer can locate the treasure at the appropriate time.

Distinctive Practices: Dzogchen

According to lineage histories of *dzogchen*, the great perfection, the system originated with Samantabhadra, who passed it on to Vajrasattva. It then entered the world of human beings and continues today in an unbroken chain of transmission. Its adherents assert that dzogchen is not a school or system of philosophy, but rather a view of reality that is based on a profound understanding of the nature of mind. It is primarily imparted through direct oral instructions of a master to a disciple, but there is also a large corpus of texts belonging to the teaching tradition and hidden treasures.

The basic text of the tradition is the *Fourfold Innermost Essence*, and the proponents of dzogchen hold that the philosophical basis of the system is the Madhyamaka view of Nāgārjuna. The lore of dzogchen was first imparted to Garap Dorjé by Vajrasattva, and then Garap Dorjé passed it on to Jambel Shé Nyen in a golden box. The teachings in the box consisted of six million four hundred thousand verses summarizing the quintessence of dzogchen.

Great perfection is the culmination of Buddhist meditative training, and the view of this system is based on the realization that appearance and emptiness interpenetrate and are inseparable. In this practice, the goal becomes the path, and one seeks to examine the fundamental nature of mind directly, without the need for images or visualizations. The *Tantra of the Great Natural Arising of Awareness* states that meditative systems which utilize images and visualizations are inferior to dzogchen, which works on the mind itself:

> Because you yourself are the divine maṇḍala,
> naturally manifest to yourself,
> Do not offer worship to the deity,
> for if you worship you will be fettered by it . . . .
> Do not renounce saṃsāra, for if you renounce it
> you will not attain buddhahood.
> Because the Buddha is not elsewhere,
> he is naught but awareness itself.
> Saṃsāra is not elsewhere;
> all is gathered within your own mind.
> Do not practise conditioned fundamental virtues,
> for if you do you will be fettered by them.
> Renounce conditioned fundamental virtues,
> such as [building] stūpas and temples.
> There is no end to contrived doctrines,
> but by leaving them they will end.
> Not renouncing the yoga of abandoning deeds,
> should you renounce deeds, you will become a tathāgata [buddha].
> So it is that you must know the path
> of the authentic buddhas in everything.[40]

Great perfection is considered by its adherents to be a practice transcending highest yoga tantra, since in the view of dzogchen even tantric visualization is only a preliminary technique of artificially creating mental images

40 Quoted in Dudjom Rinpoche, *The Nyingma School of Tibetan Buddhism: Its Fundamentals and History* (Boston: Wisdom Publications, 1991), vol. 1, 900.

which are concordant with liberation. Dzogchen, by contrast, works with the fundamental nature of the mind itself. It dispenses with mental imagery and manipulation of subtle winds and drops; instead, it aims at direct experience of the nature of mind. Great perfection also surpasses practices that aim at cultivating ethics in order to acquire good karma, since if one trains in actualizing the clear light nature of mind such actions are unnecessary.

People who become attached to "virtue" and to acquiring good karma fail to understand that the basis of transformation is the mind itself, which is of the nature of clear light. This light cannot be enhanced by the practice of virtue nor diminished by nonvirtue, and so the great perfection adept recognizes that both "virtue" and "nonvirtue" are simply conceptual constructs that ultimately constitute obstacles to realization.

Great perfection practice involves cultivating a union of essential purity (*ka dag*) and spontaneity (*lhun grub*). Essential purity refers to the mode of being (*gnas lugs*), which is emptiness. According to the view of this system, all positive qualities are spontaneously established in the sense that all are contained in the "basis-of-all" (*kun gzhi, ālaya*), the psycho-physical continuum of existence. When sentient beings realize the natural purity of the basis-of-all, this leads to attainment of buddhahood; when they fail to do so, they wander in cyclic existence.

Dzogchen Practice

The key practice of the great perfection is referred to as "cutting through" (*khregs chod*), in which yogins see through appearances to perceive the primordially pure mind. Meditators eliminate discursive thought, allowing primordial awareness to shine through mental obscurations. Through this, they learn to perceive reality from the perspective of the nondual awareness of awakened beings. The "direct approach" (*thod rgal*) involves recognizing spontaneity. In cutting through, one dissects the ego and directly trains in the primordial innate awareness without relying on appearances or signs. This is described as an effortless path, while the yoga of direct approach requires work.

Tulku Urgyen explains that cutting through is the emptiness aspect of the training and direct approach relates to use of skill in means, which allows one to master all aspects of the awakened consciousness. Cutting through eliminates ego and its permutations, while direct approach examines the manifestations that remain.[41] Both techniques are described as effortless and formless, and both are linked in this system. Mastery of cutting through enables the yogin to abide in understanding of emptiness free from all concepts. The yogin perceives the innate purity of all phenomena, and they are regarded as empty of any conceptual limitations or impurity. This banishes delusion and ignorance and reveals the true nature of reality.

Direct approach yogas enable one to comprehend that everything is innately pure. They work directly with the clear light nature of mind; the yogin views everything as naturally and spontaneously present to awareness. It is immediate realization, with no coloring by concepts or thought. It enables one to actualize all aspects of awakening in one lifetime.

Observing the Mind Itself

The primary meditative technique of great perfection is remaining in the state of pure awareness. This is accomplished by calming the mind and then abiding in comprehension of its basic clear light nature. The meditative practice involves being cognizant of the arising and passing away of feelings, emotions, sensations, etc., but understanding them within the context of pure awareness. The more one does this, the more one realizes that all phenomena arise from mind and remerge into it. They are of the nature of pure awareness and are a projection of luminosity and emptiness. Through cultivating this understanding, mental phenomena of their own accord begin to subside, allowing the clear light nature of mind to become manifest. They appear as reflections on the surface of a mirror and are perceived as illusory, ephemeral, and nonsubstantial.

Those who succeed in this practice attain a state of radical freedom: there are no boundaries, no presuppositions, and no habits on which to rely. One perceives things as they are in their naked reality. Ordinary beings view phenomena through a lens clouded by concepts and preconceptions, and most of the world is overlooked or ignored. The mind of the great perfection adept, however, is unbounded, and everything is possible. For many beginners, this prospect is profoundly disquieting, because since beginningless

41 Tulku Urgyen Rinpoche, *Rainbow Painting* (Hong Kong: Rangjung Yeshe, 1995), p. 159.

time we have been constricted by rules, laws, assumptions, and previous actions. One who is awakened, however, transcends all such limitations; there is no ground on which to stand, no limits, nothing that must be done, and no prohibitions. This awareness is bottomless, unfathomable, immeasurable, permeated by joy, unboundedness, and exhilaration. One is utterly free, and one's state of mind is as expansive as space. Those who attain this level of awareness also transcend physicality and manifest the "rainbow body" (*'ja lus*), a form comprising pure light that cannot decay, which has no physical aspects, and which is coterminous with the nature of mind.

Kagyu

The Kagyu (*bKa' brgyud*) order traces its lineage back to the Indian tantric sage Tilopa (988-1069), who is said to have received instructions directly from the Buddha Vajradhara. The name "Kagyu" literally means "teaching lineage," and its adherents claim that its doctrines and practices are passed down through a succession of awakened teachers, each of whom directly understands the true nature of reality through spontaneous, nonconceptual awareness and then transmits the essence of his or her teaching to the next generation of meditators.

Tilopa's main disciple was Nāropa, who in turn gave the teachings to Chögi Lodrö of Mar, generally referred to as Marpa (1012–1097). He is the first Tibetan member of the lineage, and he began his career as a translator of Buddhist texts. He made three visits to India in search of the dharma, and while in India met Nāropa and became his disciple. On each of his journeys, Nāropa gave him more of the teachings and initiations into tantric practices, particularly the practice of Cakrasaṃvara, the main tutelary deity of the Kagyu order. During Marpa's third trip Nāropa gave him his final instructions, including the quintessence of the great seal (*phyag rgya chen po, mahāmudrā*).

Marpa's main disciple was Milarépa (1040-1123), who is renowned throughout the Tibetan cultural area as one of the greatest figures of Tibetan Buddhism. After a series of trials he received the teachings and then spent much of the rest of his life meditating in remote areas. He had a number of famous disciples, including Réchung Dorjé Drakpa (1088-1158) and Gampopa (1079-1153). The transmission of this lineage continues today, and its vibrancy is attested to by the number of widely acclaimed lamas it has produced, including the Gyelwa Karmapas and the late Kalu Rinpoche, who was a major figure in the dissemination of this lineage to the West.

The Six Yogas of Nāropa

Among the most important practices of the Kagyupas are the "six yogas of Nāropa" (*nā ro chos drug*), which are named after the Indian master, although according to some traditions he did not develop them himself. The six yogas are: (1) heat (*gtum mo*); (2) illusory body (*sgyu lus*); (3) dream (*rmi lam*); (4) clear light (*'od gsal*); (5) intermediate state (*bar do*); and (6) transference of consciousness (*'pho ba*).

The first of these yogas (*dumo*) involves developing the ability to increase and channel inner heat through visualizing fire and the sun in various places of the body. Through training, the meditator is able to imagine her entire body being surrounded by flames, and Western medical researchers have reported significant increases in body temperature among yogins who are proficient in this practice.[42]

The technique requires the yogin to become aware, through introspective meditation, of the body's subtle energy channels and the winds that course through them. The winds are "mounts" (*rta*, literally "horses") for consciousnesses. The channels are too subtle to be perceived through dissection of the body, as are the winds.

Through meditation adepts learn to harness the energy current called "mind of awakening" and cause it to move from the left and right channels into the central channel. The yogin then causes it to rise through the cakras. This causes a sensation of increasing heat and light, which often alters bodily temperature. It is important to be aware, however, that this is not simply a substitute for warm clothing or central heating: the process is not primarily designed to produce heat, but rather to help the yogin to experience directly the luminous nature of mind.

As one works at these practices, the energy channels open and allow

42 Some interesting findings concerning the physiological effects of this practice have been reported by Dr. Herbert Benson in "Mind/Body Interactions including Tibetan Studies," in *Mind Science*, H.H. the Fourteenth Dalai Lama et al. (Boston: Wisdom Publications, 1991), pp. 37–48.

energy to flow more freely. This yoga is then combined with meditation on the nature of mind. One visualizes the subtle drop that rises through the central channel as being of the same nature as one's own mind, and through deepening this perception the drop and the mind come to be viewed as undifferentiable. Meditators who are adept at this technique also experience the subtle "pride" or dignity of being a fully awakened deity. This experience is different from ordinary pride, because it is free from false conceptuality and afflicted mental states.

A person who works at this yoga gains control over the energy channels and subtle drops, which is a necessary precondition for the other five yogas, all of which require familiarity with, and proficiency in, this mystic yoga of psycho-physical control and manipulation of energies.

The latter five yogas are based on *dumo*. When practicing them, one generally spends one-third to one-half of each session training in heat yoga and the rest with the specific techniques of each yoga.

The technique of *illusory body* begins with the insight that the phenomena of cyclic existence are mental creations. This yoga involves visualizing a subtle body that is different from the physical body, which is composed of the five aggregates. One imagines an illusory form imbued with the six perfections that is being transformed into the "vajra body" (*rdo rje'i sku, vajra-kāya*), symbolizing supreme buddhahood.

This practice is compared to the way that magicians in India were said to be able to create illusory images that appeared as concrete and real to the audiences which came to see them. In the context of the yoga of illusory body, the reason for visualizing an unreal image and imbuing it with apparent reality is to analyze whether or not it is different in essence from the phenomena of ordinary experience. Diligent analysis and meditation reveal that all phenomena are empty of inherent existence. They emerge from mind and return to it, like waves rising from water. The yogin realizes that there is no inherently real difference between his mind and the mind of a buddha, and this technique is said to be a powerful tool for quickly transforming one's ordinary consciousness into that of an awakened being.

Having gained a measure of control over the vital winds and channels, the meditator now uses subtle energies and mind to produce an illusory body in the form of a tantric deity which appears to be real, although it lacks substantial existence. It is compared to a mirror image, which seems like the thing of which it is a reflection but is completely devoid of substantial reality. Unlike the mirror image, however, the illusory body is created from subtle aspects of energy and mind that are generated as the form of the deity. The energies and mind used in this exercise should be visualized as residing at the heart as an indestructible drop. These should be thought of as the most subtle basis for the imputation of "self."

One causes the vital energies to enter the central channel, remain there for a while, and then dissolve into clear light. The clear light is then generated as a tantric deity, which means that the meditator is visualizing his vital nature and mind as a fully awakened buddha. The form of the deity enters into the clear light, and so one's vital energy and mind become the deity. This experience is a counteragent to feelings of desire and aversion, and it quickly leads to actualization of the state of Vajradhara. In addition, gaining proficiency in generating and manipulating the illusory body is essential for related exercises in the next stage, dream yoga, which utilizes similar techniques.

Dream Yoga involves taking control of one's dreams, determining their contents, and using this practice to influence the activity of mind. Ordinary people are helpless in their dreams: they are buffeted by images and emotions that are beyond their control. The tantric yogin, by contrast, learns to control dreams by manipulating the vital energies that operate during sleep. Waking perceptions are understood to have no more (and no less) veracity than images in dreams, and this yoga helps to weaken one's rigid attachment to conventional "reality."

There are two primary aspects of this yoga: (1) manipulating the contents of dreams so that they no longer reflect negative mental states but are transformed in accordance with tantric symbolism; and (2) gaining awareness of the fact that one is dreaming while one is in the dream state. In the first practice, one mentally generates tantric deities, bringing to mind the symbolism associated with them, and uses these visualizations to replace the random, afflicted images of dreams with Buddhist images and positive mental states that counteract mental afflictions.

The second aspect is closely connected, because it allows one to become aware of the dream process as it unfolds and to exercise control over it. The training begins with developing the ability to focus on the energy center (*cakra*) at the throat and visualizing a soft, glowing light there. One then cultivates this image until it becomes clearer and more radiant. This exercise is important in that it marks a measure of control over one's dreams while one is in the dream state. The next phase involves becoming aware of the unfolding of dream images and watching their arising and cessation within recognizing their illusory nature. This in turn helps meditators to determine the contents of dreams, and those who become skilled in this yoga are able to populate their dreams with buddhas, ḍākinīs, etc., thus subtly transforming their consciousnesses in accordance with these images.

In the yoga of *clear light*, the practitioner becomes aware of the nature of mind. Its luminosity is visualized as radiating out everywhere in all directions, like a lamp that illuminates both itself and other objects. The mind of clear light is seen as both an unwavering radiance that is untouched by the apparent negativities of mental afflictions and a pure, vibratory sound that encompasses all other sounds. Its luminosity is unrestricted, and its purview is universal. It is also perceived as radiant emptiness, an emptiness from which images and concepts arise, but one realizes that these are not different from mind. They are simply manifestations of the creative power of consciousness, and so one understands that they have no power in themselves.

The yogas of the *intermediate states* were described in the previous chapter. They involve simulating the process of death while still alive and applying tantric meditative techniques while in the bardo state. A person with the proper meditative training can make great progress at this time because the coarse levels of mind that normally dominate one's awareness drop away, and one actualizes very subtle states of mind that before death are only accessible to advanced meditators.

The practice of *transference of consciousness* has a number of levels, some of which are geared toward nonadepts, and others that are only attained by people who are well advanced on the path. For beginners, it is said that just receiving empowerments for this practice from a qualified lama can result in transference to a pure buddha land if one brings the teachings to mind at the time of death. After receiving the empowerment, a practitioner should develop a strong yearning for a pure buddha land and should continue to cultivate this throughout his life. If successful, at the moment of death the consciousness escapes through the "Brahmā aperture" (the fontanel, which is the place at the crown of the head where the bones of the skull meet). A person who is about to die should also repeat the mantra *hik* over and over, as this is said to aid in the process of transference.

If one is doing this while still healthy in order to practice for the time of actual death, pronouncing the mantra *hik* sends the consciousness out, and the mantra *ka* causes it to return. The process is repeated three times, and one sign of success is the appearance of a small hole (or sometimes a pustule) at the fontanel, out of which a small amount of blood or lymph flows.

Transference of consciousness empowerments are commonly given to people who wish to have an "insurance policy" when they die. By receiving the empowerments, they hope to gain rebirth in a Buddhist pure land, where the conditions are optimal for attainment of buddhahood.

All of these yogas serve to undermine attachment to the phenomena of ordinary experience as being fixed and immutable. They give the successful meditator a measure of control over the unfolding of experience and allow him to manipulate it in ways that are thought to be impossible by people still bound by the conceptual limitations of ordinary beings. Even death is no longer the inevitable cessation of existence, but rather a doorway of opportunity for spiritual progress.

Mahāmudrā, the Great Seal

There are three primary features of Kagyu tantric practice: (1) visualizing oneself as a deity and practice of sādhanas; (2) practice of inner yogas, which work with the subtle body; and (3) formless meditations, in which one rests in the nature of mind. All Kagyu schools emphasize the primacy of the great seal, which Kagyupas consider the essence of all Buddhist teachings. This essence lies not in the texts or doctrines of Buddhism, but rather in direct, personal realization of truth, which is epitomized in mahāmudrā practice.

Like the practice of great perfection (*dzogchen*) in Nyingma, the path of great seal involves directly realizing the luminous nature of mind, which leads to instantaneous self-realization. Kagyu tradition regards this as the most rapid of all paths to awakening. A meditator of sharp faculties, who diligently pursues this path, can reach awakening at any moment through directly experiencing the clear, luminous nature of mind, which in its essence is the same in buddhas and ordinary beings.

In order to penetrate the mysteries of mahāmudrā, it is necessary to find an awakened teacher, a person who has successfully traversed the path and thus acquired the ability to look directly into the minds of students and skillfully guide them past the pitfalls they will encounter in their training. The student must have a strong desire to transcend the sufferings of cyclic existence, well-developed compassion for other sentient beings, a high level of intelligence, and, most importantly, an intense and unwavering faith in the lama.

Initially the student is expected to undergo the training of the preliminary practices, which help to purify past karma and focus one's attention on the goal of awakening. This in turn brings blessings and empowerments, which serve to overcome obstacles on the path.

Great seal practice is divided into three aspects: basis, path, and result. The basis is correct understanding, which is founded on comprehending the nature of mind. The meditator quiets the mind through meditation that stabilizes it and thus begins a process of disengagement from the habitual tendencies of random, deluded thoughts. This is expanded by means of the practices of the path, which involve meditation on the nature of mind. The result is the culmination of the process, in which one actualizes the potential for buddhahood inherent in the nature of mind.

Understanding the Nature of Mind

After the student completes the preliminary practices, the next stage is cultivating calm abiding and higher insight. In the Kagyu system, the former involves a state of single-minded concentration in which one rests in the mind's natural condition of blissful, clear awareness. Higher insight in this system involves analyzing the nature of mind within the meditative state and perceiving its pure, mirrorlike nature. Like a clear mirror, it reflects what is put in front of it, but its nature is eternally unsullied and unaffected by its contents.

The path of the great seal initially involves developing positive mental qualities, which serve to counteract the negative emotions that cloud the perception of ordinary beings. One must also cultivate pure devotion to the lama; this is said to be essential to successful meditation. Through following the lama's instructions and engaging in meditation on the nature of the phenomena of experience, one finds that they are all empty of inherent existence and are merely manifestations of mind. Mind is also found to be empty, and all of its apparent contents are illusory. Through cultivating this insight, one realizes that all mental afflictions and negative mental states are empty like space, are not a part of one's own nature, and are not different from mind. When an emotion like anger arises, one looks for its basis and decides that it is a manifestation of mind, and that mind is empty, clear, and unimpeded. Thus the emotion has no independent existence and has no real claim on one's mind.

Once one begins to perceive emotions in this way, their strength diminishes, as does their motivating force. A thought or emotion is perceived as being essentially empty, a creation of mind. Mind itself is also empty, and so the emotive force is transmuted through this realization. There is no need to repress or suppress emotions, since they are nothing in themselves. The meditator should simply experience them as they appear, while subjecting them to scrutiny to determine whether or not they have any substantial reality. Thus the arising of passions and afflictions becomes an occasion for meditative practice, and even powerful negative sensations like hatred, rage, lust, etc. are transformed into unconquerable bliss through realizing their lack of inherent existence.

Effects and Benefits of the Training

Mahāmudrā adepts are particularly renowned for developing supranormal powers, which are said to result from cultivating the insight that the phenomena of experience are the play of mind. The phenomenal world is viewed as empty, as a projection of mind, and those who fully realize this are able to manifest miracles and to actually transform the phenomenal world in accordance with their wishes.

This is only possible for a person who is free from attachment to conceptual thought. As long as the mind clings to "reality" as being solid and immutable, one is limited by such conceptions. By contrast, a person who knows phenomena and mind to be of one nature of emptiness perceives them as malleable, transitory images arising from emptiness and receding again into emptiness. This state is referred to as "the union of appearance and emptiness" (*snang stong zung 'jug*).

The more one remains in this state, the greater one's equanimity becomes.

Distraction diminishes, and eventually one reaches the state of "one-pointedness," in which one is able to focus on a single thing for extended periods of time without distraction. The next important level of progress is one in which the yogin is able to engage in meditation spontaneously, with little mental effort. Simply thinking of meditation on the nature of mind is enough to bring about the experience, and awareness of the wonderful simplicity of mind pervades all the yogin's activities. This stage is termed "simplicity." One eliminates conceptual superimpositions, even such notions as existence and nonexistence. Phenomena are viewed in their most simple aspect, free from terms and concepts.

The stage of simplicity is followed by the level of "one taste," in which all of one's experiences—all thoughts, emotions, desires, etc.—are perceived as being of one taste with the essential emptiness of mind. Prior to this stage, one's equanimity is easily distracted, and one is only able to meditate for periods of a few minutes, but a yogin at the level of "one taste" can sustain meditative concentration for extended periods and apply it to all types of mental states. The perception of these as being of one taste of emptiness, and as being of the nature of mind, becomes so pervasive that one no longer has to exert any effort in meditation.

At this point, meditation becomes a spontaneous experience of the nature of mind, and one no longer even thinks of meditating. Since one is always meditating, there is no distinction between meditation and nonmeditation. As thoughts arise, they are understood to come from emptiness and return to emptiness. This level is termed "beyond meditation."

Even ordinary meditation at some point becomes a hindrance to realizing the natural, spontaneous, free flow of mind. At this point, one's meditation is effortless, and one lets go of any attachment to meditation. One cultivates the understanding that all appearances, thoughts, emotions, and forms are merged into the primordially pure truth body and that one has from beginningless time been awakened. Nothing new is added, and nothing is taken away; rather, the innate luminosity of mind asserts itself, and one abides in unshakable equanimity. One is unfettered by conceptuality, remains in the state of bliss characteristic of buddhas, and one is able to act spontaneously for the benefit of others.

The final level of attainment is a state of pure spontaneity, radical freedom of thought, and action without boundaries. All previous limitations are transcended, and there is nothing that one must do, no rules, and no set guidelines. The mahāmudrā adept perceives phenomena through naked awareness, without the mediation of presuppositions or concepts, as they are in reality. This reality has no solidity, no fixed nature, and it is utterly malleable. Reality is what one makes it, and one's freedom is absolute. This is the realm of buddhas, who transcend all limitations and develop godlike powers, the ability to know whatever they wish, and insight into the minds of other beings. Their compassionate activity for the benefit of others arises spontaneously from their nature, without planning or hesitation. While understanding the concerns of ordinary beings, they are not bound by them, and their actions are the play of the luminous nature of mind.

Sakya

The Sakya order traces its origins to India, particularly to the great adept Virūpa, who is the first human to disseminate the most distinctive of its teachings, the practices of "path and result" (*lam 'bras*; pronounced "lamdré"). The Sakya tradition in Tibet began with the establishment of a monastery in an area called Sakya, in the province of Tsang in south-central Tibet. The name "Sakya" literally means "gray earth," because the ground in this area was of gray color. Sakya Monastery was founded in 1073 by Gönchok Gyelpo (1034–1102), and with the later ascension to power of the Sakya lineage this became one of Tibet's great monastic centers. Gönchok Gyelpo was a disciple of the translator Drokmi (c. 993–1077), who traveled to Nepal and India, where he studied Sanskrit with Śāntipa, one of the great masters of his day and author of a commentary on the *Hevajra Tantra*. Drokmi brought the text to Tibet and translated it, and it later became the basic text of Sakya tantric practice.

The Khön Lineage

According to Sakya lineage histories, the Khön family (which founded and continues to direct the Sakya tradition) has its origins in the distant past, when three brothers of the heavenly race called Hla Rik descended from the Ābhāsvara heaven and landed on the peak of a salt-crystal mountain in Tibet. The two eldest brothers, Chiring and Yuring, then returned to the heavens, but Yusé, the youngest, stayed on earth with his family. His great-grandson, Yapang Kyé, married Yadruk Silima, who gave birth to a boy named Khön Bargyé. Khön Bargyé is said to be the founder of the Khön family.

For generations the Khön were closely associated with the Nyingma lineage, and Khön Bargyé's son Khön Nāgarakṣita was reportedly a student of Padmasambhava and one of the seven Tibetan "probationers" who were initiated at Samyé and became the first Tibetan monks.

The Sakya patronage of Nyingma ended when Khön Bargyé's descendant Shérap Tsültrim saw a public display of tantric ritual at a Nyingma center. Shérap Tsültrim was outraged that secret rites were being performed for the entertainment of the populace, and he felt that such public advertisement of tantric mysteries cheapened them and did immeasurable harm to people who were not prepared for them. He concluded that because of this cavalier attitude toward esoteric rites it was no longer possible for people to gain liberation through following Nyingma practices, and he decided to separate the Khön family from Nyingma.

Eschewing the older tantras favored by the Nyingmapas, he sent his younger brother, Gönchok Gyelpo, to study the new tantric translations with Drokmi. Through his studies with Drokmi and his students, Gönchok Gyelpo gained a comprehensive understanding of Vajrayāna, as well as sūtra literature and philosophical treatises. At the age of forty, having become widely recognized as one of the great Buddhist scholars of his day, he founded Sakya Monastery, which was the seat of the order until the Chinese invasion of the 1950s.

The Sakyapas became the most powerful order in Tibet in the thirteenth century when they were appointed as regents by the Mongol rulers. Because of the authority they derived from their Mongol patrons, the Sakya hierarchs were the regents of Tibet for several generations. From 1245 until 1358, they were the acknowledged rulers of the country, but just as their ascendancy was tied to the Mongols, when Mongol power diminished so did that of the Sakyapas. Their influence was greatly weakened with the death of Qubilai Khan in 1294, and Sakya hegemony ended with the collapse of Mongol control of China (1358-1360).

Distinctive Practices: "Path and Result"

The characteristic meditative system of Sakya is termed "path and result" (*lamdré*), which is a comprehensive vision of Buddhist practice based on the *Hevajra Tantra*. *Lamdré* is a shortened form of the term "path including its result," which signifies that in this system the two are held to be inseparable and not two distinct factualities. One cannot legitimately differentiate path from result, nor can result be distinguished from path; from the point of view of awakening, all such dichotomies vanish. The result subsumes the path, since the latter leads to the former; and the path subsumes the result, since it is the means whereby the result is actualized. Just as a seed contains the potential to produce a sprout if the proper conditions are present, so a qualified student has the aptitude to attain the fruit of awakening if he or she meets with the necessary conditions: the essential instructions (*gdams ngag*), an awakened teacher, tantric empowerment, and the diligence necessary to practice successfully. The result is already present in the mental continuum of the practitioner, and the path is the technique for making it actual.

In this system, the path includes the cause, because on the path one purifies the defilements that prevent actualization of awakening. The path also includes the result, because the result can only be realized through successful practice of the path. The result includes the cause, because the result is a transformed aspect of the cause. A person who attains the result makes manifest a previously unperceived aspect of the cause and dispels the misconception that they were different.

Adherents of the tradition claim that its integrity is ensured by the "four authenticities": authentic teachers, authentic direct experiences, authentic scriptures, and authentic treatises. Teachers are certified by realized masters in an unbroken chain of transmission. Their meditations, based on hearing and practice of the secret oral instructions, lead to direct perception of the truths realized by adepts of the past. The scriptures are inherited originally from buddhas and passed on to human masters, and they in turn compose treatises that explain the system for students.

According to lineage histories, it originally existed only as an oral tradition (*snyan brgyud*) which was passed on in secret by a master to a few exceptional and advanced students. Before the eleventh century, writing down the explanations and practices of path and result was not allowed, unless a disciple received special permission from his teacher.

The "Triple Appearance" and the "Triple Continuum"

An important tenet of path and result teachings is the similarity of the three aspects of the "triple appearance" (or "triple perspective": *snang gsum, tryavabhāsa*) and the "triple continuum" (*rgyud gsum, tritantra*). The triple appearance consists of: (1) the appearance of phenomena as impure error; (2) the appearance of experience in meditation; and (3) pure appearance. Lamdré texts indicate that these are fundamentally the same and that the only difference lies in how they are perceived. The triple continuum consists of basis (*gzhi, ādhāra*), path (*lam, mārga*), and result (*'bras bu, phala*). As with the parts of the triple appearance, the components of the triple continuum are fundamentally nondifferentiable. All divisions are creations of mind, and mind in lamdré is the locus of such distinctions as "basis," "path," and "result," although in itself it is luminous and empty.

In discussions of the triple continuum, the basis is said to be the two truths (conventional truths and ultimate truths), the path consists of cultivating method and wisdom, and the pure vision is the result. These are also linked to the triple appearance, since ordinary beings perceive reality in terms of conventional truth, and thus phenomena appear to them in the impure aspect. Those who are on the path engage in meditative practice in order to cultivate method and wisdom. Method involves training in love and compassion and developing the mind of awakening. The wisdom aspect focuses on meditation on emptiness. The result is the attainment of buddhahood, which is characterized by the pure vision in which one no longer perceives the distinctions of basis, path, and result, method and wisdom, ordinary beings and buddhas.

The Tibetan Appropriation of the Lamdré System

The scriptural basis of path and result, the *Hevajra Tantra*, was brought to Tibet by Drokmi, who studied with the Indian master Gayadhara (d. 1103), to whom Drokmi paid a large sum of money so that he would impart his teachings. Drokmi later returned to Tibet and translated the *Hevajra*

Tantra, which provides the guiding vision for lamdré practice. He also is credited with translating two explanatory tantras and Virūpa's *Vajra Verses*.

The *Hevajra* was viewed by the founders of the Sakya lineage as a distillation of the teachings of both sūtra and tantra, and many of the great Sakya masters wrote commentaries on it or developed liturgical cycles based on its teachings. The practice of lamdré was systematized by Drakpa Gyeltsen, who formulated an integrated system based on four primary factors: correct view of emptiness, meditation, ritual, and accomplishment. According to his system, exalted wisdom (*ye shes*) is innate, and he defines it as "clear and knowing" (*gsal zhing shes pa*). This innate exalted wisdom transcends all limiting and dichotomizing categories, such as self and other, subject and object, cyclic existence and nirvana, delusion and awakening. He further indicates that all phenomena are in fact reflections of it and have no substantial existence.

In the system formulated by Drakpa Gyeltsen, there are five primary stages in the process of gaining direct understanding: (1) initiation (*dbang*) and the interpretation (*lta ba*) of the experience produced by the initiation; (2) the generation stage (*bskyed rim*); (3) the completion stage (*rdzogs rim*); (4) training (*spyod pa*); and (5) a concluding practice that involves use of tantric seals (*phyag rgya*).

Initiation is crucial for all tantric practice, since it forges the necessary connections to tantric deities. Correct interpretation of this experience is also essential, since it aids in developing the proper orientation toward one's practice. The generation stage in this system is similar to the procedure outlined in the "Tantra" chapter: one visualizes a deity which embodies all the positive physical and mental qualities of an awakened being. The completion stage uses practices of "self-empowerment" (*rang byin brlab*), which involves heat yoga, and "maṇḍala practices" (*dkyil 'khor 'khor lo*), which include sexual yogas.

During the generation stage, one generates a mental similitude of the goal of buddhahood, transforming the mind's images into the body of a buddha within its maṇḍala, surrounded by a retinue of other deities. Everything is perceived as aspects of the maṇḍala, all sounds are heard as mantras, and all of one's thoughts are imagined to be the awakened understanding of a buddha. In the completion stage, one trains in increasing familiarity with the result. This is conjoined with the techniques of heat yoga and manipulation of winds and drops. The deities cause psychic energy to move upward through the channels. This leaves the body and fills the universe, bringing benefits to sentient beings and making offerings to buddhas and bodhisattvas. When one gains the level of control necessary to cause the winds to enter the central channel, dualistic thought vanishes. Until this point, one's perceptions will always be tinged with duality and conceptuality, and one will reflexively differentiate self and other, inner and outer, cyclic existence and nirvana.

Path and result initiates are generally first given preliminary teachings on the triple appearance and then the bodhisattva vows. Next they receive Hevajra initiation and then the full teachings of the triple appearance. Instructions on the triple continuum are reserved for students who have attained a degree of meditative accomplishment that will enable them to understand their significance.

The Inseparability of Cyclic Existence and Nirvana

The central insight of path and result is "the inseparability of cyclic existence and nirvana" (*'khor 'das dbyer med*), which is expressed in a famous verse in the *Hevajra Tantra*:

> Then the essence is described, pure and embodying wisdom, there is not the slightest difference between cyclic existence and nirvana. In the highest bliss there is no meditation and no meditator, no body, nor form, and likewise no object or subject. There is neither flesh nor blood, neither excrement nor urine, no sickness, no delusion, and likewise no purification, no lust, no anger, no delusion, no envy, no malevolence, no self-pride, no visible object. . . . The innate is calm and undifferentiated.[43]

According to this system, both cyclic existence and nirvana originate in mind (*sems*), which in its basic nature is a union of luminosity and emptiness. When mind is obscured by afflictions, there is cyclic existence, and

43 David L. Snellgrove, *The Hevajra Tantra: A Critical Study* (London: Oxford University Press, 1959), part 2, p. 39. My translation differs slightly from Snellgrove's.

when these are removed, there is nirvana. There is, however, no substantial or real difference between the two states, and so in the *Hevajra Tantra* Buddha states that all beings

> are buddhas, but this is obscured by adventitious defilements. When this is cleared away, they are buddhas at that very [moment] . . . There is no being that is not a buddha if it knows its own true nature. Hell beings, hungry ghosts, animals, gods, humans, and demi-gods—even worms on a dung-heap and so forth—have an eternally blissful nature . . .[44]

There is no real difference between the mind of a buddha, a beginner on the path, an advanced spiritual adept, or even a worm in a lump of manure. The only distinction lies in their respective perceptions of their environment: a buddha perceives reality in a manner that is free from defilements, while the consciousnesses of other beings are tainted by varying degrees of afflictions. When afflictions are removed, the causal buddha—which was previously unrecognized due to adventitious obscuration—becomes an actualized buddha, who differs from the causal buddha in terms of perception of reality.

Mind as a Union of Luminosity and Emptiness

In path and result texts the character of mind is said to be luminosity, and its basic nature is emptiness. Luminosity does not detract from emptiness, nor does emptiness undermine luminosity. Rather, the final nature of mind is an inexpressible state of union of these two factors. Mind is without beginning, middle, or end, and it transcends any attempts to limit, conceptualize, or analyze its nature.

The basis of all ordinary thoughts and conceptions is the "fundamental mind" (*gnyug pa'i sems*), which is innate (*lhan cig*) and is a union of luminosity and emptiness. All that appears to exist is nothing but a projection of the luminous nature of mind. But since the nature of mind transcends

44 Ibid., pp. 72–73.

all dichotomization or conceptualization, all appearances are viewed as illusions, as forms projected by mind with no substance.

Path and Result

In path and result practice, the characteristic of luminosity is connected with the stage of generation, since in this practice one emanates deities from the luminous nature of mind. Mind's characteristic of emptiness is linked with the completion stage, in which the images are merged with the meditator, who understands that the nature of the deities and the nature of mind are both emptiness. The exalted wisdom that results from successful practice of these two stages is the outcome of repeated familiarization. It should be noted, however, that according to lamdré masters this wisdom is not something newly produced by meditative practice; rather, meditation makes manifest the "naturally innate exalted wisdom."

In the "result" aspect of this method of training, the techniques connected with luminosity result in the ability to produce emanation bodies, and practice concerned with meditation on emptiness is connected with actualization of the truth body. The complete enjoyment body is the coincidence of both aspects.

GÉLUK

The Gélukpa order was founded by Tsong Khapa Losang Drakpa (1357-1419), one of the great figures of Tibetan religious history. A renowned scholar, meditator, and philosopher, his written work contains a comprehensive view of Buddhist philosophy and practice that integrates sūtra and tantra, analytical reasoning, and yogic meditation. He was also one of Tibet's great religious reformers, a devout monk who dedicated his life to revitalizing Tibetan Buddhism and recapturing the essence of Buddha's teachings as he understood them.

The beginning of his order can be traced to his founding of Ganden Monastery in 1410. This monastery was intended to provide a center for his reformed order of Buddhism, an order in which monks would strictly adhere to the rules of vinaya, sharpen their intellects in philosophical debate, and engage in high-level tantric practice. The school he founded was originally referred to as "Gandenpa," after its first monastery, and later became known as "Gélukpa," or "System of Virtue," in accordance with its reformist orientation.

One of the main goals of his teaching, writing, and practice was the reform of Tibetan Buddhism. He was greatly concerned with what he perceived to be lapses in monastic discipline, shoddy thinking on exoteric and esoteric topics, and a decline in tantric practice. Part of his reform program was the creation of a new order which, like its founder, has traditionally stressed the importance of strict adherence to the rules of the vinaya, the importance of comprehensive study of Buddhist thought, and reformed tantric practice that accords with the vows of monks.

The Continuation of Tsong Khapa's Tradition

Tsong Khapa's work was continued by his two greatest students, Kédrup and Gyeltsap. At the request of the other disciples, Gyeltsap ascended the throne of Ganden, indicating that he was recognized as the primary successor to Tsong Khapa's lineage. He held this position for twelve years until his death. Gyeltsap was succeeded as "Throne Holder of Ganden" by Kédrup, who retained the position for seven years until his passing at the age of fifty-four. These two lamas came to be regarded as the "spiritual sons" of Tsong Khapa and are commonly depicted sitting on either side of their master in *tanka*s and other religious paintings. The position of Throne-Holder of Ganden continues today, and the incumbent is considered to be the head of the Gélukpa order.

During the following centuries, the fortunes of Géluk rose quickly, mainly because it continued to produce an impressive number of eminent scholars and tantric adepts. Another factor in its success was its initial reluctance to become involved in Tibetan politics. Instead, for several centuries after the death of Tsong Khapa, the Gélukpa order was mainly renowned for its strict adherence to monastic discipline, its accomplished scholars, and its intensive meditative training.

This attitude of aloofness toward politics was not to last, however. As Gélukpa leaders continued to enjoy an enviable reputation for scholarship, monastic discipline, and tantric attainments, the order attracted growing numbers of novice monks and built new monasteries, such as Tashihlünpo, which was founded in 1445 by Gendün Druba. This later became the seat of the Panchen Lamas, who are second only to the Dalai Lamas in prestige in the Gélukpa order. Gélukpa monastic institutions grew and flourished, and these began to attract students from all over the Tibetan cultural area.

The Gélukpas began to acquire significant political power in the sixteenth century as a result of the discovery of the third Dalai Lama among the Mongols. This initiated a long-standing bond between the two groups.

After the defeat of the last ruler of Tsang province by Gushri Khan in 1642, the victorious khan appointed Ngawang Losang Gyatso (1617-1682), the fifth Dalai Lama, as temporal and spiritual leader of Tibet. This ensured the future supremacy of the Gélukpa order. The fifth Dalai Lama consolidated the hegemony of the Dalai Lamas, who continued to be recognized as the rulers of Tibet until the Chinese annexation of the region in 1959.

Distinctive Practices: The Stages of the Path

Perhaps the greatest legacy of Tsong Khapa was his brilliant synthesis of Buddhist doctrine and practice outlined in his two seminal treatises, *The Great Exposition of the Stages of the Path* and *The Great Exposition of Secret Mantra*. Each of these voluminous texts contains a comprehensive vision of the path to awakening that is based on the classical Indian model. In this system, the beginner is conceived of as a person whose mind is afflicted by mental defilements that prevent him or her from perceiving reality correctly. The defilements prompt ordinary beings to engage in nonvirtuous activities, and these in turn result in suffering. More importantly, ordinary beings become conditioned to such negative mental states by repeatedly engaging in nonvirtuous deeds. The key to overcoming suffering lies in eliminating the basic ignorance that blinds sentient beings to the consequences of their actions. Tsong Khapa's presentation of the path begins with beings at this level and describes their condition and its causes. He then outlines a graduated path by means of which they can overcome their afflictions, engage in virtuous actions, remove mental defilements and their predispositions, and finally, through diligent training, attain final awakening.

Tsong Khapa begins his presentation with the practices and doctrines that are common to both the sūtra and tantra systems. This is the subject matter of *The Great Exposition of the Stages of the Path*. He continues his analysis in *The Great Exposition of Secret Mantra*, which presents a graduated path to awakening in accordance with the Vajrayāna system.

The characteristic Gélukpa system of the path to awakening is referred to as "*lamrim*" (*lam rim*), "stages of the path." As this term indicates, the path is envisioned as proceeding in hierarchically arranged stages, and trainees are expected to complete each level before moving on to the next one. This is important because later trainings require successful completion of the preceding stages.

Each aspect of the path prepares the mind and alters the perceptions of trainees in ways that help them to overcome suffering and its causes. The basic problem is ignorance, and this results in a multitude of nonvirtuous actions. The only way to overcome this ignorance and the actions that result from it is gradually to wean the mind from afflicted mental states. Tsong Khapa's *Great Exposition* is a blueprint for this process.

The Three Principal Aspects of the Path

The stages of the path system is also summarized by Tsong Khapa in several shorter treatises, the most important of which is *The Three Principal Aspects of the Path*. In this work, Tsong Khapa divides the Buddhist path into three primary features: (1) the intention definitely to leave cyclic existence, (2) generating the intention to attain awakening for the sake of all sentient beings, and (3) the correct view of emptiness. These crystallize the essence of all Buddhist teachings and practices, and they are said to be the primary goals of all Buddhist sūtras, tantras, and commentaries. He indicates that these should not be viewed as partial or introductory, since they are the foundation of all practice and are as necessary for successful Vajrayāna training as they are for nontantric meditation.

The Géluk System of Tantra

Like the other three orders of Tibetan Buddhism, the Gélukpa presentation of the path contains elements of sūtra and tantra practices. All four traditions emphasize the necessity of preliminary study prior to serious meditation training. Just as one needs to know where one is going and how to get there before deciding to journey from one place to another, so Buddhist meditators must learn the outline of the path, the sorts of practices in which they will engage, and the experiences they can expect to have—along with the dangers and antidotes—and so Tibetan Buddhists who are serious about either exoteric yogas or Vajrayāna are expected to spend years learning their respective systems. Most Tibetan masters have devoted decades to scholastic training before beginning serious tantric meditation, and this approach has its antecedents in ancient India, where the monastic universities were centers both of learning and practice. Even among the *siddha* lineages, trainees generally spent many years of apprenticeship under a master's guidance before venturing into remote areas for solitary contemplation.

Like the other three orders, the Gélukpas have an extensive and highly developed system of tantric practice, which includes the training of deity yoga described in the "Tantra" chapter, the "six yogas of Nāropa," formless meditations of "great seal" and "great perfection" lineages held in common with Kagyu and Nyingma lineages, as well as distinctive techniques derived from their own sources.

The main tantra for Géluk is the *Cakrasaṃvara*, and the *Kālacakra* is also an important source for doctrine and practice. The Gélukpa tradition, like the Sakyapas, generally contends that because of the difficulty of the path and the rigors of tantric practice, one must have a thorough education in exoteric and esoteric topics prior to engaging in Vajrayāna training. Once this has been accomplished, Géluk masters emphasize the supremacy of tantra and encourage students to apply themselves to it diligently. Unlike some other Tibetan orders, the Gélukpas do not consider formless meditations by themselves to be sufficient for attainment of buddhahood: one must also master the techniques of heat yoga, illusory body, and visualization, along with long-term engagement in daily repetition of liturgical cycles (*sādhana*). Furthermore, while some orders contend that the practice of sexual yogas with a physical consort is not necessary for the attainment of buddhahood and that one may do so through visualizations alone, Gélukpa masters from the time of Tsong Khapa have contended that the subtle physiology of the winds, drops, and channels can only be transmuted into that of an awakened being through yogas involving an actual consort. On the other hand, Gélukpa tradition has tended to restrict such practices to an elite few adepts who have undergone years of rigorous training prior to receiving the instructions of sexual yoga. Most practitioners are advised to remain monks or nuns and to employ meditations in which the consort is imagined, as this is safer and more effective for the vast majority of Buddhists.

Gélukpas also emphasize the importance of frequent retreats, and like the other three orders maintain meditation centers in which trainees can engage in three-year periods of solitary contemplation after receiving a thorough grounding by their instructors. Some Western converts to other Tibetan traditions dismiss the Gélukpas as a group of scholars who neglect tantric practice, but this is a naïve and uninformed prejudice; in reality, the Gélukpas have an extensive repertoire of Vajrayāna lineages and traditions of practice going back to the origins of the system in India.[45] Its major figures were both accomplished scholars and tantric adepts, and they are revered as much for their meditative accomplishments as their learning.

It is true that Géluk has traditionally emphasized the centrality of study as a prerequisite for successful practice, but this in no way diminishes its commitment to meditation, and there is general agreement that without extensive training none of the advanced levels of the path are attainable. The Dalai Lama (who was trained in the Gélukpa scholastic system) is an example of the dual emphasis on study and practice. He spent his early years under the tutelage of senior scholars, mastering the lore of exoteric and esoteric Buddhist systems, and attained the highest level in his *géshé* examinations.[46] He is one of the greatest debaters of his generation and has an impressive knowledge of Buddhist literature. He also spends a significant

45 One of the recurring ironies of the Western appropriation of Tibetan Buddhism is a common anti-intellectual bias on the part of many newly converted enthusiasts, particularly those who do not speak Tibetan. The Tibetan lamas these converts revere generally spent decades in intensive scholastic study, and this is a prerequisite for certification as a teacher. The anti-intellectual attitude is particularly prevalent among Westerners who study with lamas from the Kagyu and Nyingma orders (but is by no means restricted to them)—who often assert that study by itself is insufficient and that one must also engage in meditation in order to attain advanced levels of realization—but they themselves received a thorough grounding in exoteric and esoteric lore as part of their training. I know of no Tibetan lamas who did not receive such instruction and simply entered solitary retreat; the idea that one might successfully meditate without any prior knowledge of the path—of Buddhist systems of meditation, of pitfalls and antidotes—would be as ridiculous to Tibetan lamas as the idea that one might decide to drive from New York to California blindfolded, simply getting into a car without consulting a map or asking directions, gunning the gas, and hoping that one might reach one's destination.

46 The *géshé* degree is the highest level of the Géluk monastic education system. Successful candidates often spend between twenty and thirty years in intensive study, which involves

part of each day engaged in tantric meditation. He receives ongoing instruction in the Vajrayāna cycles of a range of lineages, and also has tutors for the formless meditations that are most closely associated with Kagyu and Nyingma, but which also have become part of the Géluk lineage.

This is true of many other senior Gélukpa lamas, who spend years memorizing and debating the fine points of the textbooks of their respective colleges, but then expand their horizons and delve into other areas of Buddhist learning. Most also engage in tantric practice from an early age, and this is integrated into the monastic curriculum. Following the successful completion of each level of the scholastic system, students generally go into long-term solitary retreat, where their conceptual knowledge is integrated into the visualizations of deity yoga and the techniques of the order's distinctive tantric practices. Many Gélukpas decide to leave the scholastic stream at some point and become full-time meditators, and spend most of their lives in caves or meditation huts. The system recognizes that there is a range of proclivities among practitioners and has corresponding options for study and practice. All Géluk masters agree that the techniques of highest yoga tantra are the fastest and most effective means for attainment of buddhahood, and the order maintains a range of lineages, each with its particular approach and esoteric lore, and this allows Géluk teachers to accommodate different aptitudes and orientations.

---

memorization of Indian texts and works by the luminaries of the order, along with oral philosophical debate.

Lexicon of Buddhist Terms

action seal (*las kyi phyag rgya, karma-mudrā*): an actual tantric consort used in the sexual practices of **highest yoga tantra.**

action tantra (*bya rgyud, kriyā-tantra*): the tantric system that emphasizes external ritual activities (the first of the four classes of **tantra**).

aggregates (*phung po, skandha*): the components of the psycho-physical personality, on the basis of which beings commonly impute the false notion of self; the five aggregates are: form, feelings, discriminations, consciousness, and compositional factors.

arhat (*dgra bcom pa, arhat*): a person who has destroyed the mental defilements and become detached from the phenomena of **cyclic existence.**

awakening (*byang chub, bodhi*): the state of **buddhas**, in which one has awoken from the sleep of ignorance and perceives reality as it is.

bardo (*bar do, antarābhāva*): the intermediate state between death and rebirth.

bodhicitta (*byang chub kyi sems, bodhicitta*): literally "mind of awakening," the altruistic intention to become awakened in order to benefit others.

bodhisattva (*byang chub sems dpa', bodhisattva*): literally "awakening being," one who has generated **bodhicitta** and seeks awakening for the benefit of others.

bodhisattva level (*byang chub sems dpa'i sa, bodhisattva-bhūmi*): the hierarchy of stages (usually ten in number) through which **bodhisattvas** progress on their way to the state of buddhahood.

Buddha (Śākyamuni): the historical Buddha, named Siddhārtha Gautama at birth, who is credited with establishing Buddhist doctrine in the present era.

buddha (*sangs rgyas, buddha*): one who has perfected compassion and wisdom through following the **bodhisattva** path, who has become fully omniscient and has actualized the three bodies: complete enjoyment body, truth body, and emanation bodies.

cakra (*rtsa 'khor, cakra*): an energy nexus in the physiological system of **highest yoga tantra.** A cakra is a place where the left and right **channels** wrap around the central **channel** and constrict the flow of energies.

calm abiding (*zhi gnas, śamatha*): a meditative state in which one is able to focus on an internal meditative object for as long as one wishes without becoming distracted by laxity or excitement.

channel (*rtsa, nāḍī*): according to the subtle physiology of **highest yoga tantra**, the energy pathways through which subtle energies called **winds** and **drops** move. The most important of these are the central channel and channels to the left and right of it.

compassion (*snying rje, karuṇā*): sensitivity to the sufferings experienced by other beings, coupled with a desire to help them to overcome suffering and its causes.

complete enjoyment body (*longs spyod pa'i sku, saṃbhoga-kāya):* one of the three bodies of **buddhas** (the others are the truth body and emanation bodies). It is a pure form composed of light that appears to advanced **bodhisattvas.**

compositional factors (*'du byed, saṃskāra*): volitional activities, both good and bad, which influence future mental states; one of the five **aggregates.**

consciousness (*shes pa, vijñāna*): the continuum of dualistic cognition, which encompasses the six types of ordinary consciousness (eye, ear, nose, tongue, body, and mind); one of the five **aggregates.**

cyclic existence (*'khor ba, saṃsāra*): the endless cycle of birth, death, and rebirth that is based on ignorance.

deity yoga (*lha'i rnal 'byor, devatā-yoga*): the practice of visualizing a **buddha** and mentally transforming oneself in accordance with this visualization.

dependent arising (*rten cing 'brel bar 'byung ba, pratītya-samutpāda*): the process of causation, in which phenomena are created, sustained, and pass away in dependence on causes and conditions.

dharma (*chos, dharma*): (1) the teaching and practice of Buddhism; (2) a phenomenon.

discrimination (*'du shes, saṃjñā*): mental differentiations of the phenomena of experience, based on feelings; one of the five **aggregates.**

doctrine: see **dharma.**

drop (*thig le, bindu*): the subtle energies found in specific places in the body according to the **highest yoga tantra** system.

dzogchen (*rdzogs chen*): literally "great perfection," this is a meditative practice closely associated with the Nyingma order that is based on the idea that all appearances are creations of mind (which is said to be an entity of luminosity and emptiness).

emanation body (*sprul pa'i sku, nirmāṇa-kāya)*: a form created by a **buddha** for the benefit of sentient beings; one of the three bodies of a **buddha.**

emptiness (*stong pa nyid, śūnyatā*): the final nature of phenomena, their absence of inherent existence.

feeling (*tshor ba, vedanā*): sensations of things; one of the five **aggregates.**

form (*gzugs, rūpa*): things that constitute the physical world, including the senses; one of the five **aggregates.**

higher insight (*lhag mthong, vipaśyanā*): a meditative practice in which one analyzes the object of observation in order to ascertain its final nature.

highest yoga tantra (*rnal 'byor bla na med kyi rgyud, anuttara-yoga-tantra*): considered by Tibetan exegetes to be the supreme of the four classes of **tantras,** it involves visualization exercises that manipulate and transform subtle energies called **winds** and **drops.**

Hīnayāna (*theg pa dman pa, hīnayāna*): literally "Lesser Vehicle," this encompasses Buddhist teachings and practices aimed at removing mental afflictions and attaining **nirvana.**

initiation (*dbang, abhiṣeka*): a ceremony that allows a meditator to engage in the practices of a particular tantric cycle.

intermediate state: see **bardo.**

karma (*las, karma*): action (which is linked with its causes and effects).

lama (*bla ma, guru*): a spiritual preceptor.

lamdré (*lam 'bras, mārga-phala*): literally "path and result," a meditative practice closely associated with the Sakya order and based on the *Hevajra Tantra* which emphasizes the inseparability of the path and its resultant effects.

mahāmudrā (*rgya chen po, mahāmudrā*): literally "great seal," this is a meditative system closely associated with the Kagyu order that emphasizes direct realization of the luminous and empty nature of mind and phenomena.

Mahāyāna (*theg pa chen po, mahāyāna*): literally "Great Vehicle," this is the Buddhist system that emphasizes the path and practices of the **bodhisattva.**

maṇḍala (*dkyil 'khor, maṇḍala*): a diagram used in tantric meditation as an aid to visualization which represents the residence and perfected attributes of a **buddha.**

mantra (*sngags, mantra*): a ritual formula used in tantric meditation.

mind of awakening: see **bodhicitta.**

mind of clear light (*'od gsal sems, prabhāsvara-citta*): the most basic and fundamental level of mind.

New Orders (*gsar ma*): the schools whose teachings and practices are primarily based on the translations of the period of the second dissemination of Buddhism in Tibet (Sakya, Kagyu, and Géluk).

nirvana (*mya ngan las 'das pa, nirvāṇa*): the state of liberation from the sufferings of **cyclic existence.**

path and result: see **lamdré.**

path of accumulation (*tshogs lam, saṃbhāra-mārga*): the first of the five Buddhist paths, during which one amasses the collections of merit and wisdom.

path of meditation (*sgom lam, bhāvanā-mārga*): the fourth of the five Buddhist paths, during which one removes subtle traces of false conceptions of inherent existence.

path of no more learning (*mi slob lam, aśaikṣa-mārga*): the fifth of the five Buddhist paths, during which one eliminates the subtlest traces of the conception of inherent existence and attains awakening.

path of preparation (*sbyor lam, prayoga-mārga*): the second of the five Buddhist paths, marked by attainment of a union of **calm abiding** and **higher insight.**

path of seeing (*mthong lam, darśana-mārga*): the third of the five Buddhist paths, so called because one directly perceives **emptiness.**

perfections, six (*pha rol tu phyin pa, pāramitā*): the six qualities in which **bodhisattvas** train, which become the matrix of the awakened personality of a **buddha**: generosity, ethics, patience, effort, concentration, and wisdom.

performance tantra (*spyod rgyud, caryā-tantra*): tantras that equally emphasize external activities and internal yogas (second of the four **tantra** sets).

sādhana (*sgrub thabs, sādhana*): a tantric meditational ritual, generally focused on a particular deity or group of deities.

Śākyamuni (*śā kya thub pa, śākyamuni*): the historical **Buddha.**

sangha (*dge 'dun, saṃgha*): the community of Buddhist monks and nuns.

Sarma (*gsar ma*): see **New Orders.**

sentient being (*sems can, sattva*): a being that possesses **consciousness.**

six yogas of Nāropa (*nā ro chos drug*): tantric practices closely associated with the Kagyu order and traced back to the Indian adept Nāropa: (1) heat (*gtum mo*); (2) illusory body (*sgyu lus*); (3) dream (*rmi lam*); (4) clear light (*'od gsal*); (5) intermediate state (*bar do*); and (6) transference of consciousness (*'pho ba*).

skill in means (*thabs la mkhas pa, upāya-kauśalya*): the **Mahāyāna** practice of adapting the doctrine to the capacities of one's audience.

stage of completion (*rdzogs rim, niṣpanna-krama*): the **highest yoga tantra** practice in which one transforms oneself into a **buddha.**

stage of generation (*bskyed rim, utpatti-krama*): the **highest yoga tantra** practice of creating a vivid image of a deity.

suchness (*de bzhin nyid, tathatā*): the final nature of phenomena, which is equated with **emptiness.**

superior (*'phags pa, ārya*): one who has reached the **path of seeing** and is able to perceive **emptiness** directly.

sūtra (*mdo, sūtra*): a teaching attributed to the historical **Buddha.**

tantra (*rgyud, tantra*): Buddhist texts that outline the practices of the **Vajra Vehicle.**

terma (*gter ma*): "hidden treasures" concealed by Padmasambhava or his disciples.

tertön (*gter ston*): "treasure discoverers," generally reincarnations of Padmasambhava or his disciples, who find **terma.**

three jewels (*dkon mchog gsum, triratna*): the Buddha, the dharma, and the sangha (also referred to as the "three refuges").

vajra (*rdo rje, vajra*): a tantric symbol that represents the indestructible union of method and wisdom that is the goal of the tantric path.

Vajra Vehicle (*rdo rje theg pa, vajra-yāna*): the Buddhist system of practice based on texts called **tantras**, which emphasizes the practice of **deity yoga** (also called the "secret mantra vehicle" and "tantra vehicle").

wind (*rlung, prāṇa*): the subtle energies that course through pathways called **channels**, according to the system of **highest yoga tantra**.

yoga tantra (*rnal 'byor rgyud, yoga-tantra*): tantric practices that involve visualizing oneself as a tantric deity (third of the four **tantra** sets).

Bibliography

Avedon, John F. *In Exile from the Land of Snows.* New York: Knopf, 1984.

Beckwith, Christopher I., ed. *Silver on Lapis: Tibetan Literary Culture and History.* Bloomington, IN: The Tibet Society, 1987.

Benson, Herbert. "Mind/Body Interactions including Tibetan Studies." In *Mind Science,* ed. Daniel Goleman and Robert A. F. Thurman. Boston: Wisdom Publications, 1991, pp. 37-48.

Berzin, Alexander, tr. *The Four-Themed Precious Garland: An Introduction to Dzogchen,* by Longchen Rabjampa. Dharamsala: Library of Tibetan Works and Archives, 1979.

Bond, George. *The Word of the Buddha.* Colombo: M.D. Gunasena, 1982.

Chökyi Nyima Rinpoche. *The Union of Mahamudra and Dzogchen.* Kathmandu: Rangjung Yeshe, 1989.

Cozort, Daniel. *Highest Yoga Tantra: An Introduction to the Esoteric Buddhism of Tibet.* Ithaca: Snow Lion Publications, 1986.

Davidson, Ronald. *Indian Esoteric Buddhism: A Social History of the Tantric Movement.* New York: Columbia University Press, 2002.

______. *Tibetan Renaissance: Tantric Buddhism in the Rebirth of Tibetan Culture.* New York: Columbia University Press, 2005.

Doctor, Andreas. *Tibetan Treasure Literature: Revelation, Tradition, and Accomplishment in Visionary Buddhism.* Ithaca: Snow Lion Publications, 2005.

Dreyfus, Georges. *The Sound of Two Hands Clapping: The Education of a Tibetan Buddhist Monk.* Berkeley: University of California Press, 2003.

Dudjom Rinpoche. *The Nyingma School of Tibetan Buddhism.* 2 vols. London: Wisdom Publications, 1991.

Garfield, Jay, tr. *The Fundamental Wisdom of the Middle Way: Nāgārjuna's Mūlamadhyamakakārikā.* New York: Oxford University Press, 1995.

Gyaltsen, Khenpo Könchog. *The Garland of Mahamudra Practices: A Translation of Kunga Rinchen's "Clarifying the Jewel Rosary of the Profound Fivefold Path."* Ithaca: Snow Lion Publications, 1986.

Gyatso, Janet. *Apparitions of the Self: The Secret Autobiographies of a Tibetan Visionary.* Princeton: Princeton University Press, 1999.

Gyatso, Janet, and Hanna Havnevik, eds. *Women in Tibet.* New York: Columbia University Press, 2005.

Gyatso, Tenzin, H.H. the Fourteenth Dalai Lama. *Kindness, Clarity, and Insight.* Tr. Jeffrey Hopkins. Ithaca: Snow Lion Publications, 1984.

______. *Path to Bliss: A Practical Guide to Stages of Meditation.* Ithaca: Snow Lion Publications, 1991.

Haarh, Erik. *The Yarlung Dynasty.* Copenhagen: G.E.C. Gad's Forlag, 1969.

Hopkins, Jeffrey. *Meditation on Emptiness.* London: Wisdom Publications, 1983.

______. *Tantra in Tibet: The Great Exposition of Secret Mantra by Tsong-ka-pa. Part One.* London: Allen & Unwin, 1977.

______. *The Yoga of Tibet: The Great Exposition of Secret Mantra by Tsong-ka-pa. Parts Two and Three.* London: Allen & Unwin, 1981.

Kapstein, Matthew. *The Tibetan Assimilation of Buddhism: Conversion, Contestation, and Memory.* Oxford: Oxford University Press, 2000.

Karmay, Samten Gyaltsen. *The Great Perfection (Rdzogs Chen): A Philosophical and Meditative Training in Tibetan Buddhism.* Leiden: E.J. Brill, 1988.

Khetsun Sangbo Rinbochay. *Tantric Practice in Nying-ma.* London: Rider, 1982.

Klein, Anne. *Meeting the Great Bliss Queen: Buddhists, Feminists, and the Art of Self.* Boston: Beacon Press, 1995.

Lamotte, Étienne. *History of Indian Buddhism.* Louvain-la-Neuve: Université Catholique de Louvain, 1988.

Lhalungpa, Lobsang P., tr. *The Life of Milarepa: A New Translation from the Tibetan.* Boston: Shambhala, 1977; New York: Arkana, 1984.

Lhundrub, Ngorchen Konchog. *Beautiful Ornament of the Three Visions.* Ithaca: Snow Lion Publications, 1991.

Powers, John. *History as Propaganda: Tibetan Exiles versus the People's Republic of China.* New York: Oxford University Press, 2004.

Ray, Reginald A. *Secret of the Vajra World: The Tantric Buddhism of Tibet.* Boston: Shambhala, 2001.

Rhie, Marylin, and Robert Thurman. *Wisdom and Compassion: The Sacred Art of Tibet.* New York: Harry N. Abrams, 1991.

Richardson, Hugh E. *Tibet and Its History.* Boulder and London: Shambhala, 1984.

Ruegg, David Seyfort. *The Life of Bu ston Rin po che with the Tibetan Text of the Bu ston rNam thar.* Serie Orientale Roma 34. Rome: Istituto Italiano per il Medio ed Estremo Oriente, 1966.

Samuel, Geoffrey. *Civilized Shamans: Buddhism in Tibetan Societies.* Washington: Smithsonian Institution, 1995.

Schopen, Gregory. *Buddhist Monks and Business Matters: Still More Papers on Monastic Buddhism in India.* Honolulu: University of Hawai'i Press, 2004.

______. *Figments and Fragments of Mahāyāna Buddhism in India: More Collected Papers.* Honolulu: University of Hawai'i Press, 2005.

Shakabpa, Tsepon W.D. *Tibet: A Political History.* New Haven: Yale University Press, 1967; reprint, New York: Potala, 1984.

Simmer-Brown, Judith. *Dakini's Warm Breath: The Feminine Principle in Tibetan Buddhism.* Boston: Shambhala, 2001.

Snellgrove, David L. *Indo-Tibetan Buddhism: Indian Buddhists and Their Tibetan Successors.* 2 vols. Boston: Shambhala, 1987.

Snellgrove, David L., and Hugh E. Richardson. *A Cultural History of Tibet.* London: Weidenfeld and Nicolson, 1968; Boulder: Prajna Press, 1980.

Sogyal Rinpoche. *The Tibetan Book of Living and Dying.* San Francisco: Harper, 1992.

Stearns, Cyrus. *Luminous Lives: The Story of the Early Masters of the Lam 'Bras Tradition in Tibet.* Boston: Wisdom Publications, 2001.

Thondup, Tulku. *Buddha Mind: An Anthology of Longchen Rabjam's Writings on Dzogpa Chenpo.* Ithaca: Snow Lion Publications, 1989.

English-Tibetan-Sanskrit Glossary

Terms

abhidharma (*chos mngon pa*)
action (*'du byed kyi las, saṃskāra-karma*)
action seal (*las kyi phyag rgya, karma-mudrā*)
action tantra (*bya rgyud, kriyā-tantra*)
affliction (*nyon mongs, kleśa*)
afflictive obstructions (*nyon mongs pa'i sgrib pa, kleśa-āvaraṇa*)
aggregate (*phung po, skandha*)
aging and death (*rga shi, jarāmaraṇa*)
amban (*am ban*)
antidote (*gnyen po, pratipakṣa*)
appearance of experience in meditation (*ting 'dzin nyams kyi snang ba, samādhyanubhavābhāsa*)
appearance of phenomena as impure error (*ma dag 'khrul pa'i snang ba, aśuddhabhrāntyavabhāsa*)
arhat (*dgra bcom pa*)
assumptions of bad states (*gnas ngan len, dauṣṭhulya*)
awakening (*byang chub, bodhi*)
bardo (*bar do, antarābhāva*)
bodhicitta (*byang chub kyi sems*)
bodhisattva (*byang chub sems dpa'*)
bodhisattva level (*byang chub sems dpa'i sa, bodhisattva-bhūmi*)
bodhisattva vehicle (*byang chub sems dpa'i lam, bodhisattva-mārga*)
bönpo (*bon po*)
buddha (*sangs rgyas*)
buddhahood (*sangs rgyas nyid, buddhatva*)
cakra (*rtsa 'khor*)
calm abiding (*zhi gnas, śamatha*)
channel (*rtsa, nāḍī*)
character (*mtshan nyid, lakṣaṇa*)
clear light (*'od gsal, prabhāsvara*)
clear light of death (*'chi ba'i 'od gsal*)
compassion (*snying rje, karuṇā*)
complete enjoyment body (*longs spyod pa'i sku, saṃbhoga-kāya*)
compositional factors (*'du byed, saṃskāra*)
concentration, perfection of (*bsam gtan gyi pha rol tu phyin pa, dhyāna-pāramitā*)
consciousness (*shes pa, vijñāna*)
contact (*reg pa, sparśa*)
correct aims of actions (*yang dag pa'i las kyi mtha', samyak-karmānta*)
correct effort (*yang dag pa'i rtsol ba, samyag-vyāyāma*)
correct livelihood (*yang dag pa'i 'tsho ba, samyag-ājīva*)
correct meditative stabilization (*yang dag pa'i ting nge 'dzin, samyak-samādhi*)
correct mindfulness (*yang dag pa'i dran pa, samyak-smṛti*)
correct realization (*yang dag pa'i rtog pa, samyak-saṃkalpa*)

correct speech (*yang dag pa'i ngag, samyag-vāc*)
correct view (*yang dag pa'i lta ba, samyak-dṛṣṭi*)
cutting through (*khregs chod*)
cyclic existence (*'khor ba, saṃsāra*)
ḍākinī (*mka' 'gro ma*)
death (*'chi ba, maraṇa*)
deity (*lha, deva*)
deity yoga (*lha'i rnal 'byor, devatā-yoga*)
dependent arising (*rten cing 'brel bar 'byung ba, pratītya-samutpāda*)
dharma (*chos*)
direct approach (*thod rgal*)
discipline (*'dul ba, vinaya*)
discrimination (*'du shes, saṃjñā*)
divine pride (*lha'i nga rgyal, deva-māna*)
doctrine (*chos, dharma*)
dream yoga (*rmi lam rnal 'byor, svapna-yoga*)
drop (*thig le, bindu*)
dzogchen (*rdzogs chen*)
effort (*brtson 'grus, vīrya*)
eightfold noble path (*'phags pa'i lam yan lag brgyad, āryāṣṭāṅgamārga*)
emanation body (*sprul pa'i sku, nirmāṇa-kāya*)
empowerment (*dbang skur, abhiṣeka*)
emptiness (*stong pa nyid, śūnyatā*)
energy pathways (*rtsa, nāḍī*)
essential purity (*ka dag*)
ethics (*tshul khrims, śīla*)
exalted wisdom (*ye shes, jñāna*)
exertion (*rtsol ba, vyāyāma*)
faculties, five (*dbang po, indriya*)
faith (*dad pa, śraddhā*)
feeling (*tshor ba, vedanā*)
first dissemination (*snga dar*)
form (*gzugs, rūpa*)
form body (*gzugs sku, rūpa-kāya*)
generation stage (*bskyed rim, utpatti-krama*)
generosity (*sbyin pa, dāna*)
géshé (*dge bshes*; short for *dge ba'i bshes gnyen, kalyāṇa-mitra*)
grasping (*len pa, upādāna*)
great compassion (*snying rje chen po, mahākaruṇā*)
great perfection (*rdzogs pa chen po*)
great seal (*rgya chen, mahāmudrā*)
guru (*bla ma*)
guru yoga (*bla ma'i rnal 'byor*)
harmonies with awakening, thirty-seven (*byang chub kyi phyogs, bodhi-pakṣa*)
hearer (*nyan thos, śrāvaka*)
heat yoga (*gtum mo, caṇḍālī*)
hell (*dmyal ba, naraka*)
hell beings (*dmyal ba, nāraka*)
hidden (*gab pa*)
hidden treasures (*gter ma*)
higher insight (*lhag mthong, vipaśyanā*)
highest yoga tantra (*rnal 'byor bla na med kyi rgyud, anuttara-yoga-tantra*)
humans (*mi, manuṣya*)
hungry ghosts (*yi dwags, preta*)
ignorance (*ma rig pa, avidyā*)
illusory body (*sgyu lus, māyā-deha*)
impermanence (*mi rtag pa, anitya*)
incarnate lama (*sprul sku, nirmāṇa-kāya*)
indestructible drop (*mi gzhigs pa'i thig le*)
individual liberation (*so sor thar pa, pratimokṣa*)
innate (*lhan cig, sahaja*)
inseparabilty of cyclic existence and nirvana (*'khor 'das dbyer med*)
intermediate state (*bar do, antarābhāva*)
jewels, three (*dkon mchog gsum, triratna*)
karma (*las*)
lama (*bla ma, guru*)
lamdré (*lam 'bras*)
laxity (*bying ba, laya*)
liberation (*thar pa, mokṣa*)
mahāmudrā (*rgya chen po*)
mahāyoga (*rnal 'byor chen po*)
maṇḍala (*dkyil 'khor*)
mantra (*sngags*)
mantra vehicle (*sngags lam, mantra-yāna*)
meditation (*bsgom pa, bhāvanā*)
meditational deity (*yi dam, iṣṭa-devatā*)
meditative equanimity (*btang snyoms, upekṣā*)

meditative equipoise (*mnyam bzhag, samāhita*)
meditative stabilization (*ting nge 'dzin, samādhi*)
mental factor (*sems 'byung, caitta*)
merit (*bsod nams, puṇya*)
method (*thabs, upāya*)
method continuum (*thabs rgyud*)
Method Vehicle (*Thabs kyi theg pa, Upāya-yāna*)
mind (*sems, citta*)
mind of awakening (*byang chub gyi sems, bodhicitta*)
mind of clear light (*'od gsal sems, prabhāsvara-citta*)
mindfulness (*dran pa, smṛti*)
monastery (*dgon pa, araṇya*)
monastic discipline (*'dul ba, vinaya*)
Mongol (*Hor pa*)
mount (*rta, aśva*)
name and form (*ming gzugs, nāma-rūpa*)
nature truth body (*ngo bo nyid chos sku, svabhāvika-dharma-kāya*)
New Schools (*gSar ma*)
ngöndro (*sngon 'gro, pūrvagama*)
Ngorpa (*Ngor pa*)
nirvana (*mya ngan las 'das pa*)
noble truths, four (*'phags pa'i bden pa rnam bzhi, caturāryasatya*)
nonaffirming negative (*med 'gag, prasajya-pratiṣedha*)
nonconceptual (*rtog med, nirvikalpa*)
nonsectarian (*ris med*)
no-self (*bdag med, nairātmya*)
object of observation (*dmigs pa, ālambana*)
obstructions to omniscience (*shes sgrib, jñeya-āvaraṇa*)
Old Translation School (*sNga 'gyur*)
one-pointedness (*rtse gcig pa, ekāgra*)
ordinary being (*so so'i skye bo, pṛthagjana*)
pacifying (*zhi bar byed pa, śamana*)
parinirvāṇa (*yongs su mya ngan las 'das pa*)
path (*lam, mārga*)
path and result (*lam 'bras, mārga-phala*)
path continuum (*lam rgyud*)
path including its result (*lam 'bras bu dang bcas pa*)
path of accumulation (*tshogs lam, saṃbhāra-mārga*)
path of liberation (*rnam grol lam, vimukti-mārga*)
path of meditation (*sgom lam, bhāvanā-mārga*)
path of no more learning (*mi slob lam, aśaikṣa-mārga*)
path of preparation (*sbyor lam, prayoga-mārga*)
path of seeing (*mthong lam, darśana-mārga*)
patience (*bzod pa, kṣānti*)
perfection (*pha rol tu phyin pa, pāramitā*)
perfection of aspiration (*smon lam gyi pha rol tu phyin pa, praṇidhāna-pāramitā*)
perfection of concentration (*bsam gtan gyi pha rol tu phyin pa, dhyāna-pāramitā*)
perfection of effort (*brtson 'grus kyi pha rol tu phyin pa, vīrya-pāramitā*)
perfection of ethics (*tshul khrims kyi pha rol tu phyin pa, śīla-pāramitā*)
perfection of exalted wisdom (*ye shes kyi pha rol tu phyin pa, jñāna-pāramitā*)
perfection of generosity (*sbyin pa'i pha rol tu phyin pa, dāna-pāramitā*)
perfection of patience (*bzod pa'i pha rol tu phyin pa, kṣānti-pāramitā*)
perfection of power (*stobs kyi pha rol tu phyin pa, bala-pāramitā*)
perfection of pure awareness (*rig pa tshad phebs*)
perfection of skill in means (*thabs la mkhas pa'i pha rol tu phyin pa, upāya-kauśalya-pāramitā*)
perfection of wisdom (*shes rab kyi pha rol tu phyin pa, prajñāpāramitā*)
perfection vehicle (*phar phyin theg pa, pāramitā-yāna*)
performance tantra (*spyod rgyud, caryā-tantra*)

phenomenon (*chos, dharma*)
pliancy (*shin tu sbyangs pa, praśrabdhi*)
preliminary practices (*sngon 'gro, pūrvagama*)
primordial buddha (*dang po'i sangs rgyas, ādi-buddha*)
prostration (*phyag 'tshal*)
pure land (*dag zhing, kṣetra-śuddhi*)
pure vision (*dag snang*)
rainbow body (*'ja lus*)
realm (*khams, dhātu*)
refuge (*skyabs 'gro, śaraṇa-gamana*)
renunciation (*nges 'byung, niḥsaraṇa*)
result (*'bras bu, phala*)
sādhana (*sgrub thabs*)
saṃsāra (*'khor ba*)
sand maṇḍala (*rdul phran gyi dkyil 'khor*)
sangha (*dge 'dun*)
Sarma (*gSar ma*)
seal (*phyag rgya, mudrā*)
secret mantra vehicle (*gsang sngags kyi theg pa, guhya-mantra-yāna*)
self (*bdag, ātman*)
sexual union (*sbyor ba*)
six yogas of Nāropa (*Nā ro chos drug*)
skill in means (*thabs la mkhas pa, upāya-kauśalya*)
spontaneity (*lhun grub, anābhoga*)
stage of completion (*rdzogs rim, niṣpanna-krama*)
stage of generation (*bskyed rim, utpatti-krama*)
stūpa (*mchod rten*)
suchness (*de bzhin nyid, tathatā*)
suffering (*sdug bsngal, duḥkha*)
superior (*'phags pa, ārya*)
sūtra (*mdo*)
sūtra vehicle (*mdo'i theg pa, sūtra-yāna*)
tantra (*rgyud*)
tantric empowerment (*dbang skur, abhiṣeka*)
terma (*gter ma*)
tertön (*gter ston*)
textbook (*yig cha*)
throne holder of Ganden (*dGa' ldan khri pa*)
time-lock formula (*gtsug las khan*)
transference of consciousness (*'pho ba, saṃkrama*)
truth body (*chos sku, dharma-kāya*)
truth of suffering (*sdug bsngal bden pa, duḥkha-satya*)
truth of the cessation of suffering (*'gog bden pa, nirodha-satya*)
truth of the origin of suffering (*kun 'byung bden pa, samudaya-satya*)
truth of the path (*lam bden pa, mārga-satya*)
union of appearance and emptiness (*snang stong zung 'jug*)
union of calm abiding and higher insight (*zhi gnas dang lhag mthong gi zung 'brel, śamatha-vipaśyanā-yuganaddha*)
vajra (*rdo rje*)
vajra vehicle (*rdo rje theg pa, vajra-yāna*)
vehicle (*theg pa, yāna*)
very subtle mind (*shin tu phra ba'i sems*)
vinaya (*'dul ba*)
vow (*sdom pa, saṃvara*)
wind (*rlung, prāṇa*)
wisdom truth body (*ye shes chos sku, jñāna-dharmakāya*)
yoga tantra (*rnal 'byor rgyud*)
yogin (*rnal 'byor pa*)

Personal Names

Amitābha (*'Od dpag med*)
Ānanda (*Kun dga' bo*)
Aśoka (*Chos rgyal Mya ngan med*)
Atiśa [Dīpaṃkara Śrījñāna](*Jo bo rje*)
Avalokiteśvara (*sPyan ras gzigs*)
Cakrasaṃvara (*'Khor lo bde mchog*)
Channa (*'Dun pa*)
Chöbar (*Chos 'bar*)
Chögi Lodrö (*Chos kyi bLo gros*) of Mar (*Mar pa*)
Dharmakīrti (*Chos kyi grags pa*)
Dorjé Drak (*rDo rje brag*)
Dorjé Gyelpo (*rDo rje rgyal po*)
Drakpa Gyeltsen (*Grags pa rGyal mtshan*)
Drigum Tsenpo (*Gri gum bTsan po*)
Drokmi (*'Brog mi Lo tsā Shākya Ye shes*)
Dromdön (*'Brom ston pa rGyal ba'i 'byung gnas*)
Düsong (*Dus srong*)
Gadong oracle (*dGa' gdong chos skyong*)
Gampopa (*sGam po pa*)
Gangchen (*Kang chen*)
Garap Dorjé (*dGa' rab rDo rje, Surativajra*)
Gayadhara (*Ga ya dha ra*)
Gélukpa (*dGe lugs pa*)
Gendün Druba (*dGe 'dun Grub pa*), first Dalai Lama
Gendün Gyatso (*dGe 'dun rGya mtsho*), second Dalai Lama
Gompo Namgyel (*mGon po rnam rgyal*)
Gönchok Gyelpo (*dKon mchog rGyal po*)
Gönchok Jikmé Ongpo (*dKon mchogs 'Jigs med dBang po*)
Gorampa Sönam Senggé (*Go ram pa bSod rnams Seng ge*)
Great Vehicle (*Theg pa chen po, Mahāyāna*)
Guhyasamāja (*gSang ba 'dus pa*)
Günga Gyeltsen Bel Sangpo (*Kun dga' rGyal mtshan dPal bZang po*)
Gyasa (*rGya bza'*)
Gyeltsap Darma Rinchen (*rGyal tshab Dar ma Rin chen*)
Gyelwa Karmapa (*rGyal dbang Kar ma pa*)
Hashang Mahāyāna (*Hwa shang Ma ha ya na*; Chinese: *Heshang Moheyan*)
Heruka (*Khrag thung*)
Heruka Cakrasaṃvara (*Khrag thung 'Khor lo bde mchog*)
Hevajra (*Kye rdo rje*)
Hīnayāna (*Theg pa dman pa*)
Hla Rik (*Lha rigs*)
Hlasang (*Lha bzang*)
Indrabhūti (*Indra bhu ti*)
Jambel Gyatso (*'Jam dpal rGya mtsho*), eighth Dalai Lama
Jambel Shé Nyen (*'Jam dpal bShes gnyen, Mañjuśrīmitra*)
Jamgön Kongtrül (*'Jam mgon Kong sprul bLo gros mTha' yas*)
Jamyang Kyentsé Ongpo (*'Jam dbyangs mKhyen brtse dBang po*)
Jangchup Gyeltsen (*Byang chub rGyal mtshan*)
Jangchup Ö (*Byang chub 'Od*)
Jétsun Drakpa Gyeltsen (*rJe btsun Grags pa rGyal mtshan*)
Jikmé Lingpa (*'Jigs med gLing pa*)
Jñānasūtra (*Ye shes mdo*)
Jowo Rinpoché (*Jo bo Rin po che*)
Kadampa (*bKa' gdams pa*)
Kagyu (*bKa' brgyud*)
Kālacakra (*Dus kyi 'khor lo*)
Kāṇha (*Ka ṇha*)
Karma Kagyu (*Karma bKa' brgyud*)
Karma Lingpa (*Kar ma gLing pa*)
Karmapa (*Karma pa*)
Kauṇḍinya (*Kau ṇḍi nya*)
Kédrup Jé (*mKhas grub rJe*)
Kelsang Gyatso (*bsKal bzang rGya mtsho*), seventh Dalai Lama
Khön (*'Khon*)
Khön Bargyé (*'Khon Bar skyes*)
Khön Nāgarakṣita (*'Khon Nāgarakṣita*)
Kutsang Rinpoché (*Ke'u tshang Rin po che*)
Lekbé Shérap (*Legs pa'i Shes rab*)

Lha Totori Nyentsen (*Lha Tho tho ri gNyan btsan*)
Lokakṣema (*'Jig rten bde ba*)
Lokeśvara (*'Jig rten dbang phyug*)
Longchen Rapjampa (*kLong chen Rab 'byams pa*)
Losang Tséwang (*bLo bzang Tshe dbang*)
Madhyamaka (*dBu ma*)
Mahāyāna (*Theg pa chen po*)
Maitreya (*Byams pa*)
Mañjuśrī (*'Jam dpal*)
Marpa (*Mar pa*)
Middle Way School (*dBu ma, Madhyamaka*)
Milarépa (*Mi la ras pa*)
Mipam Gyatso (*Mi pham rGya mtsho*)
Mūla-Sarvāstivāda (*gZhi thams cad yod par smra ba*)
Nāgārjuna (*kLu sgrub*)
Nairātmyā (*bDag med ma*)
Nāropa (*Na ro pa, Naḍapāda*)
Néchung oracle (*gNas chung chos skyong*)
Ngawang Belden (*Ngag dbang dPal ldan*)
Ngawang Günga (*Ngag dbang Kun dga'*)
Ngorchen Günga Sangpo (*Ngor chen Kun dga' bZang po*)
Nyatri Tsenpo (*gNya' khri bTsan po*)
Nyingma (*rNying ma*)
Padmasambhava (*Pad ma 'byung gnas*)
Panchen Lama (*Paṇ chen bla ma*)
Pudön (*Bu ston*)
Réchungpa Dorjé Drakpa (*Ras chung pa rDo rje Grags pa*)
Rinchen Sangpo (*Rin chen bZang po*)
Sachen Günga Nyingpo (*Sa chen Kun dga' sNying po*)
Śākya (*Śā kya*)
Sakya Paṇḍita Günga Gyeltsen Bel Sangpo (*Sa skya Paṇḍita Kun dga' rGyal mtshan dPal bzang po*)
Sakya Trizin (*Sa skya Khri 'dzin*)
Śākyamuni (*Śā kya thub pa*)
Samantabhadra (*Kun tu bzang po*)
Śāntarakṣita (*Zhi ba 'tsho*)
Śāntipa (*Śān ti pa*)
Sékhar Chungwa (*Se mkhar Chung ba*)
Shakya Chokden (*Śā kya mchog ldan*)
Shangdön Chöbar (*Zhang ston Chos 'bar*)
Shérap Tsültrim (*Shes rab Tshul khrims*)
Siddhārtha Gautama (*Don grub Gau ta ma*)
Sönam Gyatso (*bSod nams rGya mtsho*), third Dalai Lama
Śrī Siṃha (*Shri sing ha*)
Subhūti (*Rab 'byor*)
Śuddhodana (*Zas gtsang ma*)
Tārā (*sGrol ma*)
Tenzin Gyatso (*bsTan 'dzin rGya mtsho*), fourteenth Dalai Lama
Tilottamā (*Thig le mchog ma*)
Tri Songdetsen
Trinlé Gyatso (*'Phrin las rGya mtsho*), twelfth Dalai Lama
Tsangyang Gyatso (*Tshangs dbyangs rGya mtsho*), sixth Dalai Lama
Tsarchen Losel Gyatso (*Tshar chen bLo gsal rGya mtsho*)
Tsarpa (*Tshar pa*)
Tsenpo Khoré (*bTsan po 'Khor re*)
Tsong Khapa Losang Drakpa (*Tsong kha pa bLo bzang Grags pa*)
Tupden Gyatso (*Thub bstan rGya mtsho*), thirteenth Dalai Lama
Upāli (*Nye bar 'khor*)
Vairocana (*rNam par snags mdzad, Bai ro tsa na*)
Vajradhara (*rDo rje 'chang*)
Vajrapāṇi (*Phyag na rdo rje*)
Vajrasattva (*rDo rje sems dpa'*)
Vajrayoginī (*rDo rje rnal 'byor ma*)
Vimalamitra (*Dri med bshes gnyen*)
Virūpa (*Bi rū pa*)
Yaśodharā (*Grags 'dzin ma*)
Yéshé Tsogyel (*Ye shes mTsho rgyal*)
Yönden Gyatso (*Yon tan rGya mtsho*), fourth Dalai Lama

Locations

Amdo (*A mdo*)
Bodh Gaya (*Bodhgayā*)
Bugyel (*sPu rgyal*)
China (*rGya nag*)
Chong Gyé (*'Phyong rgyas*)
Densatil (*gDan sa mthil*)
Desire Realm (*'Dod khams, Kāma-dhātu*)
Dhanakośa (*Da na ko sha'i mtsho gling*)
Drébung (*'Bras spungs*)
Dri River (*'Bri chu*)
Form Realm (*gZugs khams, Rūpa-dhātu*)
Formless Realm (*gZugs med khams, Ārūpya-dhātu*)
Ganden (*dGa' ldan, Tuṣita*) heaven
Ganden (*dGa' ldan*) Monastery
India (*rGya gar, 'Phags yul*)
Jokhang (*Jo khang*)
Kailasha (*Ti se, Kailāśa*)
Kangchen (*Gangs can*)
Kapilavastu (*Ser skya'i gnas, Kapilavastu*)
Kham (*Khams*)
Kumbum (*sKu 'bum*)
Lhasa (*Lha sa*)
Lumbinī (*Lumb'i tshal*)
Marpori (*dMar po ri*)
Nālandā (*Nālendra*)
Nālendra (*Nā lendra*)
Néchung (*gNas chung*)
Ngor Éwam Chöden (*Ngor E waṃ Chos ldan*)
Norbulingka (*Nor bu gling ka*)
Podrang (*Pho brang*)
Potala (*Po ta la*)
Rājagṛha (*rGyal po'i khab*)
Ramoché (*Ra mo che*)
Rasa (*Ra sa*)
Sakya (*Sa skya*)
Samyé (*bSam yas*)
Sarnath
Séra Monastery (*Se ra dGon pa*)
Tuṣita (*dGa' ldan*)
Ü (*dBus*)
Vaiśālī (*Yangs pa can*)
Varanasi (*Wā rā ṇa si, Chos skor gnas, Vārāṇasī*)
Vikramaśīla (*Rnam gnon tshul*)

Titles of Works Mentioned

Blue Annals (*Deb ther sngnon po*), by Gö Lotsawa (*'Gos lo tsā ba*)

Cakrasaṃvara-tantra (*'Khor lo bde mchog rgyu*)

Compendium of All Knowledge (*Shes bya kun khyab*), by Jamgön Kongtrül

Compendium of the Truth of All Tathāgatas (*De bzhin gshegs pa thams cad kyi de kho na nyid bsdus pa'i mdo, Sarva-thatāgata-tattva-saṃgraha*)

Diamond Sūtra (*rDo rje gcod pa'i mdo, Vajracchedikā-sūtra*)

Fourfold Innermost Essence (*sNying thig ya bzhi*)

Great Exposition of Secret Mantra (*sNgags rim chen mo*), by Tsong Khapa

Great Exposition of the Stages of the Path (*Lam rim chen mo*), by Tsong Khapa

Guhyasamāja-tantra (*gSang ba 'dus pa'i rgyud*)

Hevajra-tantra (*Kye rdo rje rgyud*)

History of Buddhism (*Chos 'byung*), by Pudön (*Bu ston*)

Innermost Essence of the Great Expanse (*kLong chen snying thig*)

Kālacakra-tantra (*Dus kyi 'khor lo rgyud*)

Lamp for the Path to Awakening (*Byang chub lam gyi sgron ma, Bodhipathapradīpa*), by Atiśa

Lives of the Eighty-Four Adepts (*Caturśīti-siddha-pravṛtti*)

Official Edict (*bKa' shog*)

Perfection of Wisdom in Eight Thousand Lines (*'Phags pa shes rab kyi pha rol tu phyin pa brgyad stong pa'i mdo, Aṣṭasāhasrikāprajñāpāramitāsūtra*)

Refutation of Errors regarding Secret Mantra (*sNgags log sum 'byin*)

Secret Basic Essence Tantra (*sGyu 'phrul gsang ba snying po'i rgyud, Guhya-mūla-garbha-tantra*)

Statement of Ba (*sBa bzhed*)

Sūtra Turning the Wheel of Dharma (*Chos kyi 'khor lo rab tu bskor ba'i mdo, Dharmacakrapravartana-sūtra*)

Tantra of the Great Natural Arising of Awareness (*Rig pa rang shar chen po'i rgyud*)

Three Principal Aspects of the Path (*Lam gtso rnam gsum*), by Tsong Khapa

Translations of Teachings (*bKa' 'gyur*)

Translations of Treatises (*bsTan 'gyur*)

Vajra Verses (*rDo rje tshig rkang, Vajra-gāthā*), by Virūpa

Index